YOU CAN BE RIGHT OR YOU CAN BE MARRIED®

LOVE-BASED SOLUTIONS FOR COUPLES™

Brett R. Williams

ISBN 0-9761269-0-7

You Can Be Right Or You Can Be Married is a registered trademark of Brett R.
Williams. *Love-Based Solutions For Couples* and *The Practice of Love* are service marks
of Brett R. Williams.

Book design by Paul McNeese, OPA Consulting
Cover design by Gregg Dudics, GDArtworks

Tapas Publications
P.O. Box 5626
Huntington Beach, CA 92615-5626

Table of Contents

Dedication
Acknowledgments
Introduction: The 3 Rs of Change

Dedication

**To my loving wife, Lynda,
and our two wonderful boys,
Wesley and Trevor.**

Acknowledgments

Thanks to the clients and couples I have seen over the years, courageous men and women who have bravely and honestly opened their lives and willingly embraced the practice of love. It was their participation that helped create these love-based solutions.

Thanks also to those who worked so selflessly in the production of this book. I have been blessed with such friends and colleagues as Barbara Carbone, Heather Tarlow-Edwards, and Paul Lewis, who have assisted in editing. A heartfelt thank you also goes out to Paul McNeese for his assistance in editing, formatting and packaging, and to Gregg Dudics for the cover design.

Finally, I want to express my gratitude for those who have inspired and taught me about love. I am grateful for my father, who exemplifies love in his relationships, and to my favorite author, Adi Da, whose wisdom teaching and has revealed love's true form. Lastly, praise goes to my first spiritual master, Jesus Christ, who laid the foundation for a practice of love.

Introduction -
The 3 "Rs" of Change

You Can Be Right
Or
You Can Be Married

"Can couples married less than ten years understand that?" Most people love the title of this book, but one man was concerned that without the experience of years of marriage some would not recognize the importance of the phrase "you can be right or you can be married."

It is true that wisdom is born through experience, but many relationships do not survive the test of time. The average life span of a marriage is between four and seven years, which means that most couples do not have the time or patience to struggle before finding the insight and understanding they need.

The title, *You Can Be Right Or You Can Be Married*, encapsulates the core issue behind every couple's conflict. Disputes emerge over the kids, sex, money, and in-laws, but these quarrels eventually deteriorate into what I call a Right Fight. These battles over blame divert a couple's conversation to who is right and who is wrong. Until these Right Fights are disengaged, the deeper feelings of hurt or frustration that started their spats will never be addressed.

This book will strive to provide clarity into your disagreements and to propose solutions that go beyond simple communication. You will discover that Right Fights are not about *being right,* but about *feeling wronged.* The ultimate core of a couple's conflict is a feeling of being unloved. When we are feeling hurt or unloved by someone we love, we tend to withdraw our love. It is this "recoil" from relationship that makes communication impossible. Without a common connection between them, couples are continually misinterpreting, misunderstanding, and mis-communicating. Prior to finding the "right" words, then, two people need first to re-connect so as to establish a common ground from which to converse.

It is your wounds, not your words, which prevent you from sharing, and it is love, not language, which will be the solution. By employing techniques that restore a couple's feeling of relatedness, the divisive nature of any dispute can be disarmed.

Once a pair has reunited, many of their differences disappear. Those that remain are addressed "in love." The law of love states that we must love our neighbor as we love ourselves. When two people follow this governing principle they are able to talk freely about their upsets. By complying with the law and speaking "in love," a couple's conversation will create intimacy rather than destroy it.

Three Parts to Change and Three Sections to the Book

There are three stages involved in producing the kind of change that will improve the ways in which you deal with your spouse, raise your children, or even enhance your golf game. In the name of simplicity (and to de-personalize the discussion), let's use golf as an example.

To better my golf scores, the first thing I would do is hire an expert golf instructor, a professional who would watch me take a few shots and point out what I was doing wrong. The pro might tell me, "You're bending your elbow on your back swing." Then he would show me how to keep my arm straight. After providing a few pointers, the pro would encourage me to practice repeatedly until the behaviors become natural. From that point on, it would be my responsibility to remain conscious of the problem and to use these new skills in making it right.

These "3 Rs"—*Recognizing* what's wrong, *Refocusing* on what's right, and *Reinforcing* through practice—divide the process and this book into three logical parts.

The first four chapters will describe the problem with our relationships: namely, Right Fights.

Once we understand what is wrong, we can move on to the second section, which explains how to make things right. Here, *love* will be offered as the cure to our conflicts.

The third section provides concrete exercises that may be used for practicing these new behaviors. This third segment will actually be split into two subsections: first, learning how to love our partner; and second, learning how to love ourselves.

Section One

RECOGNIZING
What's Wrong

Chapter 1

The Right Fight

Recognizing a theme to our conflicts

The Drill

Early in my marriage I decided to play "man of the house" and get my hands dirty on a few home projects. Lynda and I had inherited an old wooden coffee table that needed to be refinished. It looked like an easy job and seemed like a reasonable place to start.

After buying a new drill and some sanding disks from the hardware store, I pulled the table outside and began sanding. Thirty seconds into the project, the drill gave out. My first reaction was, "What kind of cheap drill is this?"

After another quick trip to the store to exchange the drill, I began again. A moment later, the second drill died. "Now, that's strange. Could I be doing something wrong?"

Once more I took the drill back to the hardware store and soon returned with a third drill. This time I was extremely careful not to press too hard or overwork the drill. Despite all my precautions, within 60 seconds the drill stopped working. I had been careful to follow instructions—to do everything right. "It couldn't be me," I thought.

Next, I figured it was the brand of drills. Spending the extra money, I moved up in quality. This was to be my final attempt. The first few seconds were tense. After about a minute I began to relax. "Well, this may finally work!" Suddenly . . . silence. For the fourth time, the drill just quit!

Frustrated, I gave up the whole project. Packing the drill away in storage and covering the table with a tablecloth, I pretended that the entire incident had never happened.

That was the end of doing home projects. Since I could not figure out what was wrong, I could not make it right. First I thought it was *the drill*. Then I thought it was *my doing*. After that, I blamed the brand. Finally, when I ran out of blame objects, I just stopped analyzing the problem and put it all away.

Six months later, I was hanging around the house and a thought came to me (having given up home projects, I had more time to think.) Something told me to look at the plug I had used with the drills. I had never noticed it before, but there was only one socket in the outlet. Most residential electrical outlets have two plugs, but this had just one. "Hmmm," I mused, "the outlet is here between the front door and the front window. Window!? I wonder if that's for an air conditioner."

In the blink of an eye it all came together. The 220-ampere circuit, had pumped twice as much electricity into the drills as they could handle. Once I became aware of that fact, everything made complete sense. I instantly knew what was wrong, what the problem was, and I understood how to solve it.

Until we know what's wrong,

we can't make it right.

As embarrassing as it is to tell that story, it is a good illustration of the principle that there can be no meaningful change without first understanding the source of a difficulty. The problem I had with the drills was that I did not recognize what was going wrong. I was so busy—and upset—focusing on the "symptoms" that I did not comprehend the core mistake. Without a sense of what was going wrong, it was difficult—no, impossible—to make it right.

The same logic applies to our relationships. Without first achieving an understanding of a problem there can be no meaningful solution. Hence, the primary task in creating change in a marriage is to understand what is not working.

No Recognition = No Change

There are literally tens of thousands of self-help "relationship" books on the market today, each touting its own brand of advice. As dissimilar as each one appears, they all follow essentially the same course. The reader enthusiastically implements the exercises and activities suggested, and for a time the relationship improves. Within a few days, weeks, or months, however, the techniques stop bearing fruit and the relationship returns to a state of dissatisfaction.

As good as the book's suggestions may have been, a step was forgotten along the way. It is not enough just to change behavior; understanding must change, as well. When a couple does not completely comprehend why their relationship is failing, no change will remain effective in the long run.

Change involves three stages:

1. recognizing what is wrong,
2. learning what is right and why, and *finally*
3. practicing new behaviors.

My youngest son, Trevor, demonstrates a wonderful example of this process. Trevor is learning to do addition with regrouping. He is able to add, but he gets into trouble by forgetting to carry over. One evening, when I was looking over his homework, I noticed that he had written "28 plus 25 equals 43." It was true that eight and five were thirteen, but he had failed to carry the one over to the tens column. That was why he came up with 43 and not 53. After pointing out his error and why it affected the outcome, I showed him what he needed to do, watched him do it, then followed up with a few more practice problems.

If Trevor had not both seen and understood his mistake, none of his answers would ever have been correct. He needed to learn what he was doing wrong—and why it was wrong—before he could make it right. That is the fundamental process every couple needs to learn.

The reason our changes do not remain permanent is because we do not completely understand what is wrong in the first place. Let us look at the divorce rate as the first case in point.

Despite all the resources offered to couples through books, therapy, churches, and television programming, the divorce rate in America remains one of the highest in the world. Divorce for first-time marriages runs between 50 to 67%, depending upon which study one consults[i]. Some people believe that these high percentages are only a passing trend. Unfortunately, the numbers have been on the rise for the past 30 years.

What about those who do not divorce? It is hard to believe that every couple that decides to stay married (for the kids or for financial or religious reasons) has a satisfying relationship. There are no studies that quantify what percentage of married couples that stay together are happy, but it follows logically that at least half of those who do remain married are dissatisfied. At best, some of these unhappy couples are able to create a cordial coexistence, but that does not define a successful relationship.

If we were to add into the equation those who are unhappily married, we would see that somewhere between 75% and 83% of all marriages fail to maintain a bond of love. That translates into approximately 90 million people in the U.S. who are dissatisfied with their relationships.

These statistics point to a problem that goes far beyond the simplistic idea that a few of us picked the wrong person. The individual personality of our mate is not at issue. If only it were that simple! The divorce rate would be much less if it was just the result of some kind of personality clash. The high percentage of unhappy marriages points to a problem that, 1) extends beyond any idiosyncratic characteristics of a particular couple, and 2) the majority of people do not comprehend as a fundamental and global issue and, therefore, lack the understanding that would make them capable of doing something about it in their own cases.

Whatever is wrong is affecting all of us. Until we see this big picture, until we understand what is breaking down for every couple, we will not be able to change it.

Psychology Does Not Recognize the Problem

Even more frightening is the fact that psychotherapists, psychologists, and counselors do not seem to understand where our marriages are breaking down. There is much blame passed around. Some therapists focus on our parents, while others try to address our communication skills. Dr. John Gray and others like him look at the differences between men and women as the culprit behind our conflict. Medical doctors blame our biochemistry and seek to treat the relationship through medication. However, none of these areas of emphasis has produced any kind of significant change. One-half to two-thirds of all marriages still end in divorce.

In fact, there is a significantly higher rate of divorce for those who go to counseling than for those who do not[ii]. Of course, that is not a completely fair observation. The same statement might be made about hospitals. Given that more people die in hospitals than at home, it can be said you are more likely to die if you seek treatment than if you do not. All the same, the effectiveness of marital therapy is arguably disappointing.

When couples are asked about the benefits of counseling, they typically say that it was helpful 80 to 100% of the time[iii]. Yet, when these self-reported studies are excluded and researchers examine actual measurable changes in how often couples fight or whether or not they divorce, marital therapy seems to be effective only about 35% of the time.[iv]

One-year follow-up has found that of those who did benefit, ¼ to ½ of them eventually reverted to their old patterns. This means only 11 to 18% of couples that attend counseling are able to maintain any kind of lasting change[V]. The data suggest that psychotherapists are not any closer to understanding what is going wrong in our relationships than anyone else.

So what is going wrong? To blame our divorce rate on our parents and say that our childhood scarred us in such a way that it makes relating difficult would imply that most of the population came from dysfunctional homes. That is simply not the case.

Marriages are no longer prearranged.

We picked our partners. We married because we enjoyed his company, loved her sense of humor, and believed he was willing and able to take care of our needs. To blame our divorce on our partner would mean that neither one of us knew our mate before we wed. Perhaps a better explanation would be that something about marriage changes people.

In counseling, one third of clients stay the same, one third get worse, and one third get better. Of the one third that get better, half fall back.

To say we simply cannot communicate is an oversimplification. Couples used to be able to talk. Something changed. Marriage does seem to change people, but it not only changes our partner, it changes us. The question is, what causes these changes and why?

One Problem/One Fight

As bad as these statistics look, the good news is that our problem is quite simple. Recognizing what is wrong is not a complicated task because there is only one conflict. There is only one fight. If you could listen to any of the 120 million married people in the United States, you would hear thousands of troubling issues being discussed. However, these individual topics eventually boil down to a single conflict. It is what I call our Right Fights.

Couples clash over any number of issues, but at its root, every disagreement—whether it is about not taking the trash out or how the other person takes care of the kids—is fundamentally *a battle over blame*. Regardless of which issue starts a disagreement, the bickering eventually ends up in a dispute over *who is the good guy and who is the bad guy*. Regardless of ethnicity, age, income, or the number of years a couple has been married, every disagreement eventually becomes a Right Fight.

Open Cupboards

A classic example comes from my own relationship. The conflict in this case was over the kitchen cupboards. Lynda has a habit of leaving the cupboards ajar. It seemed as though every time I walked into the kitchen I had to close all the cabinets. No sooner would I turn around than they would all be open again. Normally, would hold my tongue and shut the cabinets—again and again. One Friday evening, though, I was too tired to hold back, "Why can't you close the damn cupboards?!"

Lynda heard the irritation in my voice as a personal attack. To her it meant, "Why can't you do anything right?"

Offended by my comment, she lashed back. "Why can't you remember to close the back gate when you leave?"

I am not sure why, but I was surprised at her reaction. Perhaps I expected her to say, "Oh, thank you for yelling; I'll try to do better in the future." Yet, silly as it sounds, there was a part of me that expected exactly that. So when she responded by attacking me, I felt doubly hurt. Here I was, venting about something I thought was legitimate, and she not only ignored my complaint but also attacked me in return. It felt as though she was telling me that I did not have a right to get upset about the cupboards.

"If I left the gate open as many times as you leave the cabinets open, then maybe you could make that comparison," I retorted. I had every right to complain (I thought), and her analogy was completely unfair.

The conversation was doomed from the start. Why? Because it was never really about cabinets. The focus was not on the issue but on which of us was the bad guy. The issue of cupboards being open was twisted into one of me criticizing of Lynda for denying my right to be angry. In that moment, each of us became defensive; *the conversation shifted from open cupboards to who has the right to be upset and who does not.*

Lynda could have turned to me and said, "OK, I'll close the cupboards," but it would not have made a bit of difference. Her closing the doors was no longer the point. My agenda had become to prove her wrong, not only for leaving the cabinets open but also for "attacking" me when I was expressing my frustration.

Lynda was hurt by my attack, too, yet rather than to express her pain she shifted the focus to me and that *I* was the one with the problem. Lynda saw my yelling as being "out of line." She saw me as critical and condescending. She was not going to quit until she got me to acknowledge my transgression. Like two kids on the playground, our partner's poor behavior became the justification for our own assaults. "He (she) hit me first!"

~

Wes got upset when Liz returned from the market having forgotten to buy razor blades. Liz became frustrated that he did not appreciate the time and energy it takes to shop for the family. Liz got mad when Wes would not stop to ask directions. Wes would get angry when Liz would imply that he was lost.

~

As you can see, different topics set us off, but it always comes back to the same basic argument: who is right and who is wrong.

The issues that ignite our confrontations seem endless—from leaving socks on the floor, to how much was charged on the credit card, to differing sexual appetites. Regardless of how they start, most arguments eventually disintegrate into a *Right Fight*.

Exercise - "He Said, She Said"

Consider any conflict, be it yours or a friend's, or even a disagreement you witnessed between strangers, and listen for the Right Fight. Using a sheet of lined paper, make two columns. On the top of the left hand section write the title "She Said," and on the right hand side write the title "He Said." Now go through the disagreement line by line and summarize what each person expressed in the appropriate column. If you are the wife, put what you said in the first column, followed by your husband's response on the opposite side. List back and forth what each of you said in the proper side.

The example below contains several common disagreements to illustrate how to briefly encapsulate each other's remarks.

She said -

"You don't listen."

"Why do you always go out with your friends?"

"Can't you help with the kids?"

"I'm sick of you controlling the money."

He said -

"You don't stop talking."

"There's nothing wrong with my friends."

"Nothing I do is right."

"You spend too"much."

Analysis of the Example

After the details are written out, go back and read over your list of accusations and listen to what is really being said. "You don't listen" clearly translates to "You're wrong for not listening." The retort back, "You don't stop talking," shifts the problem back to the other person. "Why do you always go out with your friends?" implies there is something wrong with him going out. His response, "There is nothing wrong with my friends," communicates the message "I have a right to leave for awhile. It is you who has the problem."

The intent may be to communicate frustration at not getting any help with the kids, but it sounds like "You're wrong for not helping." The return comment, "Nothing I do is ever right," seems to indicate that the focus is on him, but the message is "You're the problem because you're never satisfied." In the last two jabs about money, the objective is to point out how the other person handles the finances is "wrong."

The message of "I'm right" is also communicated in the above statements, but it takes a little deeper listening in order to hear it. The communication about being right takes two forms. It is either conveyed as "I do it the right way," or it comes out as "I have a right to my feelings and needs." Let us again use the above statements as our example.

The complaint about not listening is usually given by the person in the relationship who values communication. Therefore, when she says, "You don't listen," what is meant is, "I enjoy communicating, I am normal. If you don't, then you have a problem." The reverse is also true. The non-communicators are the ones who grumble about excessive speech. "I don't need to talk about everything, why do you?" The attitude is, "I'm right because I don't have to talk all the time."

The statement about going out was shared by someone who valued staying home. Therefore embedded in her critique was the message "you should be a homebody like me". His comment, "There is nothing wrong with my friends," let his partner know he has a right to do what he wants, and again she is wrong to try to change him. The other gentleman who comments, "Nothing I do is ever right," believes he was entitled to sit and relax. Finally, the woman who complains, "I'm sick of you controlling the money," lets her spouse know she has a right to spend as she sees fit.

None of these examples specifically accuse the other as being wrong, nor directly states that we were right, but the message is there all the same. When we say, "I am right," we are making our partner wrong. In turn, by pointing out where he/she was amiss, we infer we have it together.

Change first involves recognizing what is going wrong with our communications. So right now, spend 10 to 15 minutes and find the message of "I'm right and you're wrong" in your own dialogues. Go over your exercise and make sure you hear how both of you are communicating both messages.

Defining a Fight

Many couples do not like to "fight." Instead, they avoid. A word or two is expressed and then the conversation is dropped. No one screams. Voices are not raised. The conversation may often not last more than a minute. There are even times when neither party will say anything. They will just walk away from each other. Those who avoid rather than argue often believe they do not have conflicts. The truth is, disagreements can occur without either person ever saying a word.

These "cold wars" are just as dangerous and destructive to a relationship as the verbal assaults. When a couple divorces, it is often because they have grown apart. The pair feels like roommates. The marriage is dissolved not because they are having daily screaming matches but because they have become strangers. The opposite of love is not anger, it is apathy (or an absence of feelings).

So let us back up for a moment and define an argument. Any interaction between two people that results in creating distance is a fight. Notice that definition does not limit our disagreements to yelling matches. In fact, it extends it to situations in which one or both parties leave feeling disconnected, removed, or estranged.

These silent conflicts are less destructive in the short run. For the longer term, however, if the distance is never bridged and the relationship is left disconnected, a relationship will eventually dissolve. The unresolved issues pull the couple apart even without a word being said.

~

"What are you going to make for dinner?" Larry had been home, so Heather hoped he could put something together for the family.

Larry replied, "I don't know. What do you want?"

Because Heather wanted Larry to be responsible for the entire meal, including deciding what to make, she did not offer any suggestions. She simply finished the conversation. Once she walked in the door and found that he had done absolutely nothing, she did what was needed to get the meal ready, yet she pointedly had nothing to do with Larry for the rest of the evening. Feeling her cold shoulder, Larry withdrew as well.

~

No harsh words were exchanged, yet it was a fight all the same. Even without words, the core of their conflict was a *Right Fight*. She believed she had a right to ask Larry to make dinner, and she felt he was wrong not to do so. To Larry, on the other hand, it was Heather who was unreasonable. He would have made dinner, if she had given him a plan. He believed that he was right and that she was wrong to have been so angry.

Most marriages do not explode in a burst of flames. Instead, couples drift apart. They fall out of love, feeling more like roommates than lovers. Their unresolved conflicts produce distance. Open psychic wounds create walls that at first protect but eventually divide. Couples who report that they never fight (in the yelling sense) are still vulnerable to divorce when the two are emotionally estranged by their conflict.

There Is a Right and Wrong

There are moral truths in the world, but these "truths" are not what couples are fighting about. The differences that are at the core of conflicts are often the petty issues of who did or said what. The "right" and "wrong" in any discussion is like "right" and "left"—it is a self-reference, which depends upon your own unique and individual perspective on a situation.

Example: On my right there is a bookcase, while for you—since you are facing me—the bookcase is on your left. In the same way, "right" and "wrong" also depend upon point of view. They are expressions of personal experience and comprehension.

Instead of seeing right and wrong in this relative way, couples get in trouble when each partner believes his or her own point of view to be absolute, constant, indisputable truth, like north and south. When right and wrong are seen not as individual beliefs but as universal truth, then people become "righteous".

There may be moral absolutes in life, but how to load the dishwasher or whether or not to spend time with your in-laws are not included in those immutable truths. If we are talking politics or parenting problems, when one or both parties takes the attitude that their point of view is only point of view, conflict will be the inevitable result.

The Reason Marriages Fail

Step one to change is: knowing what is not working. In marriage, the malfunction usually is that couples become trapped in Right Fights. As human beings we all have to express upset, hurt, irritation, and disappointment in order to have a meaningful relationship. However, the battle over blame can take a couple off topic and prevent the healing activity of sharing feelings or needs. The reason marriages fail is not because spouses experience a few negative emotions. Rather, it is because the issue of right and wrong sidetracks the conversation and prevents the sharing of pain and frustration.

Homework: Journal every fight during the next week. Use the same format as the "He said/She said" exercise. Focus on recognizing the emotional messages you have hidden in the conflict. There is no change without first recognizing what is not working. Therefore, spend some time this week looking at yourself and seeing what you are doing to exaggerate your conflicts.

Chapter 2

"I Don't Want
To Be Right . . .
I Just Don't Want
To Be Wronged!"

Why we do not recognize our Right Fights

The White Sheep

I was the "white sheep" in my family. Most kids go through a rebellious period in which they try to find themselves by rejecting what their parents and society tells them. I was an adolescent in the mid '70s, and we were living in California, where everyone around me was drinking and using drugs—including my own family. Mom was deep in her alcoholism and drug addiction, and my brothers were going through their experimental drug phase. Even my minister father would dabble occasionally. Rebelling, for me, meant not using drugs and, instead, living life on the straight and narrow.

My "rebellion" did not produce a lot of friction with my father, but it did create conflict between me and my oldest brother, Dave. Being the white sheep, I was forever correcting David, our family black sheep.

Our sibling rivalry flared up frequently with me calling him a loser and him calling me self-righteous—and then kicking my butt.

I never took much stock in his comments. Being self-righteous was never what I intended. I simply wanted him to help with household responsibilities. In my view, somebody who was self-righteous was also self-centered and self-absorbed. Those traits sounded more like David than me. Bottom-line, it seemed as though he labeled me as righteous in order to avoid looking at himself.

Then I grew up and got married. After a year or so, Lynda began to accuse me of "always needing to be right." That hurt, but I quickly deflected it. Again, it was never my intent, nor was it how I saw myself. Her remarks came after I pointed out what she did that hurt or bothered me. Hence, I compared her remarks to those my brother would make and saw her accusation of my being righteous as her way of avoiding responsibility.

As the years passed, I found there was a price for not looking at my role in our arguments. Lynda and I became distant. Our conflicts taught me there were no winners, only losers. As I realized the futility of our fights, it left me with only one other choice: avoid friction by avoiding Lynda. This decreased our confrontations, but increased the feelings of isolation.

As long as I thought it was David and Lynda who were not taking responsibility, I never realized that *I* needed to become accountable. Only when I took off the blinders that prevented my seeing my part in our Right Fights did I become empowered to create change.

Let us go deeper into this recognition process by: 1) revealing what blinds us from seeing our Right Fights; and 2) exposing the core or source of these battles over blame.

No One Sees It

The whole idea of being able to organize all fights into one central theme is simple, clean, and very usable. The only problem is that no one "gets" it. Well, that is, literally, a half-truth. Each member of a couple easily recognizes how the other is engaging in a Right Fight. The trouble is that neither recognizes that he/she is doing the same.

~

Stephanie and Russ came into my office fighting about how to handle Kevin, their 16-year-old. Stephanie shared that she saw Russ as distant and aloof. "The only time he comes out from behind his paper is to yell at Kevin. It's no wonder Kevin doesn't listen. Russ never takes the time to build a relationship."

It came as no big surprise to me that Russ did not see things in quite the same way. He thought Stephanie needed to be "more like a parent and worry less about being Kevin's friend."

When I asked if they knew what they were really fighting about, all they could see was the issue with Kevin. The moment I suggested that the issue might be about who was right and who was wrong, both of them immediately grasped the concept.

"Oh, yeah, he can't stand being wrong. He never admits he made a mistake or says he is sorry." Stephanie could easily see that this argument was not over Kevin. It was about Russ' need to prove that his way was the right way. In essence, she began recognizing that every fight either involved Russ pushing to be right or making her wrong. However, when she was asked to look at her part, it was a bit more difficult for her to see her contribution to creating their disagreements. "I don't need to be right."

Russ quickly volunteered to help Stephanie with examples of how she needed to be right. "The only way I can get her to drop the issue is to admit that she was right and I was wrong." Russ's struggle in our discussion was in identifying when and how he also got "stuck" on being right.

~

The exchange above provides a typical example of how people are able to recognize the Right Fight as something their partner is doing, but they usually miss how they are participants in the process.

Not About A Negative Personality Trait

The blame we place on our partner is what prevents us from seeing our role in our disputes. "Well, I didn't start the fight, she did." Our failure to see our part in our disagreements stems from our belief that we did not initiate the clash.

In any quarrel, the common perception is that the participants each play one of two roles—the "perpetrator" or the "victim." The aggressive "perpetrator" is generally believed to have spawned the confrontations and so is responsible for the fight. The "victim" is seen as the unfortunate recipient of the attack and, therefore, is not liable for the conflict. That does not mean the one who is assaulted is necessarily passive. The "victim" may also be brutal in his/her counter-offensive because it is in self-defense.

The distinguishing characteristic is that the innocent "victim" accepts no accountability for the attacker's behavior. The *perpetrator* is the one who is responsible for a given conflict. The *victim* is merely protecting himself/herself.

The problem with this perception is that in most conflicts, there is never a perpetrator, only victims.

In most conflicts there are

only victims, no perpetrators!

Tom woke up late. As he hurriedly tried to get dressed, he blurted out, "Where are my damn socks?"

Hearing the anger in his voice, Arlene replied, "Well, if they aren't in your drawer, then you probably didn't put them in the dirty clothes to get washed."

Tom then retorted, "I don't know why you have to use this moment to get in your digs. Can't you just help me get ready?"

Arlene defended herself. "I am not the one who started fighting, you are. Don't blame me for the fact that you're late."

~

What is interesting in this example is that research shows that each participant in a conflicted relationship sees themselves in the role of victim[vi]. Given a choice, every spouse would choose to view himself/herself as the one being assaulted—and their partner as the assailant.

This was clearly the situation with Tom and Arlene. If you asked who was attacking and who was defending, both of them would report they were only protecting themselves because their partner was the one who struck first.

Arlene interpreted Tom's harsh tone to imply that he was angry with her. The issue was more than Tom blaming her for his tardiness. Arlene believed Tom was calling her a "bad wife," and there was simply no way to let that go.

Tom did not come back with, "Okay, point well made, I'll make sure I pick up my socks." He was hurt, and he wanted to hurt her in return. Tom's reaction stemmed from the same sense of annoyance, as did Arlene's. Already frustrated about being late, he assumed that Arlene's comment was unsupportive.

The fact was that neither was in the wrong. Tom was not attacking her, he was frustrated. Although Tom believed that Arlene was at fault for her poorly timed criticism, it was not Arlene's intention to give a dig. She felt that she had to explain why the socks were not in the drawer. Arlene was convinced that Tom was wrong for attacking her and also unfair for not taking responsibility for his tardiness or, for that matter, his irritability. As always, there were two victims and no perpetrators.

We believe that the person who started the fight is the perpetrator—the responsible party—while the victim is blameless. Of course, since all of us are victims it is difficult for an involved party to see how he or she could be responsible for these Right Fights.

The truth, though, is just the opposite. Right Fights are not the evil creation of a perpetrator. Instead, they stem from the defensive position of victims. The very fact that we see ourselves as victims, as the ones who have been wronged, makes *us* the good guy, and, in turn, *our partner* the bad guy. The concept of right and wrong is introduced by the person who sees himself or herself as being hurt.

No One Intends To Fight

Have you ever listened to yourself on tape? Your voice sounds odd to you because what you hear is what others hear when you speak to them, not what you hear inside your own body. Literally, you do not hear yourself in the same way as do those around you.

The same is true for your conversations. Because your ideas roll around inside your own head, they sound one way to you, but at times they may be heard very differently by those with whom we are speaking.

In any conversation, there is a distinction between *intent* and *content*. As a conceptual example, *intent* may be compared to the items we have written down on our grocery list, while the *content* is what is in our cart. Sometimes we may leave out some items that are on our list, and other items not on the list may somehow find their way into the shopping cart. So our shopping *intent* may not match our shopping *content*.

The *intent* of a message is what someone means to say, while the *content* is the words that are actually spoken. In other words, what we wish to say may not always be exactly what comes out.

It is difficult for us to see how our content somehow becomes focused on "good guy" and "bad guy," because that was not our intent. Couples generally do not intend to make their partners wrong, nor is it their intent to make themselves right. The real intent is to share our feelings, express our frustrations, convey our needs, and somehow restore the relationship, but our good intentions prevent us from hearing our attacks.

Exercise- Two Pens / Two Messages

An exercise that can help us to become aware of the difference between our intent and our content is to write it out. Think of some event or situation that bothered you. Take as much time and paper as needed to completely express all the issues that contribute to your feelings of "upset."

Then, using two different colored highlighters, go through the entry and mark in one color what you are *feeling*. Focus on the actual issues: "My feelings were hurt when . . ." or "I am bothered about . . ." In the other color, highlight your partner's transgression. "You said . . ." or "You never . . ."

Look over everything you have written down and notice which color dominates. Despite your intent, the dominant color on the page reveals your content. If the marker representing all your feelings dominates, then your content and intent match. This indicates your communications are clear and consistent with what you intend to say. When the dominant color on the page emphasizes your partner's behavior, then what you think you are saying does not agree with what was, indeed, being expressed.

This means that even though you really desire to share your pain, in reality all you are doing is attacking your partner. Further, this means you are perpetrator, not victim.

Right Fights Are about Feeling Wronged

Ultimately, Right Fights are not about being right, they are about feeling wronged. Couples have trouble recognizing their battles over blame for two reasons:

1) They are aware of their good intentions.

2) They see being right the same as being righteous.

For example, at some time during the day, one partner may have done something (or not have done something) or said something (or not have said something) that caused the other partner to feel hurt. Because the pain came from a loved one, the hurt is compounded, and the offended partner feels slighted, wronged, and unloved. Any resulting communication then becomes an attempt to defend against the perceived injustice that seems to have been done, and the objective of the communication is to right that wrong.

In a general sense, it is not so much that we want to be right. Rather, it is that we do not want to be wronged or hurt by our partner. Our Right Fights are about defending what we see as our *right* to feel upset and/or to point out what the other person did *wrong* so that he/she will not do it again.

The problem is pain, not pride. The instinctive response to feeling wronged causes a re-focusing of intention, thus producing a fight about who is right. Potentially then, the blame game may arise in any relationship.

Homework: Identifying the core of your conflicts. Take out your list of Right Fights from the last homework assignment, the "He said, She said" exercise.

Go back over what you were distressed about. Look for the core issue, or wound, that started the conflict. If it was about not having sex, then ask yourself, "Why is it a problem my partner does not want to be intimate?" If the dispute was over a lack of communication, do the same thing. "Why is it problematic that my spouse does not like to talk?"

As you write down these answers you will begin to see that behind every disagreement there is a feeling of being hurt or wounded. For instance, the fact that two parents discipline their children differently is not a problem. The problem is that both of them feel hurt by their partner's lack of support.

Chapter 3

Who's Wrong vs. What's Wrong

The problem is, we fail to communicate

Crumbs

One Saturday morning I was sitting at the kitchen table eating breakfast when Lynda entered the room. Immediately, she began complaining about the mess I had made. "Am I the only one who cleans up around here? Can't you wipe off the cutting board after you make something?"

My first thought was, "Why is she on my back?" It was not that I was going to leave it there. Lynda's comment felt like an attack.

I then tried to share my feelings. Unfortunately, whenever I express my hurt, it looks a lot like anger. "What's the big deal? It is just a few crumbs. I'll get them when I am done." I did not say that I was right, and she was wrong, but that was definitely the implication.

She responded, "The big deal is that I worked all evening Friday cleaning, and first thing Saturday morning I wake up to your mess. The big deal is that you don't help to keep the house clean."

I tried convincing her of the logic behind my behavior. "If I clean up first, my toast would get cold." The words were correct, but the tone carried the added message, "What a stupid suggestion."

Reading my wife's body language is not my forte, but the glare she gave me as she stormed out of the room left me with the impression that she did not get my point. Lynda had missed the beauty of my argument.

Chasing her down the hall, I continued, with a pathetic blend of apology and justification, "I'm sorry, but I just don't see why you're making this such a big deal."

"Whatever!"

That was her final remark as she slammed the bedroom door in my face.

Some would say Lynda and I were having a "communication problem." I disagree. Lynda and I were expressing ourselves quite well. Both of us made our points crystal clear. There was no misunderstanding as to what the other was saying. Neither Lynda nor I struggled to find the words. The problem was in the "unspoken" message. Our difficulties started when we got stuck on "who's wrong" versus "what's wrong."

Most couples converse effectively. Conflicts arise because our Right Fights shift our discussions. The blame game takes us off topic. We are not having trouble communicating; our mistake is that we are "correcting" the other party. Let us examine the anatomy of arguments and demonstrate how battles over blame can prevent a couple from conversing and, instead, shift the communication into a correcting mode—and perhaps even into a combative stance.

What's Wrong vs. Who's Wrong

To understand our Right Fights we need to understand the difference between "what's wrong" and "who's wrong." *What* is wrong is the *fact* that we are hurt, angry, sad or afraid. *Who* is wrong revolves around the issue of *who should take responsibility* for creating those negative emotions.

Simply stated, our Right Fight shifts the conversation from a discussion about feelings to one that is focused on behavior—*specifically, the other person's behavior.*

Lynda was hurt. After working all day Friday, she had come home and, instead of resting, she had worked hard at getting the house straightened up and cleaned. Waking up the next morning only to find crumbs on the counter made her believe that all her hard labor had been for naught. When she found the kitchen a mess, she felt unloved.

Notice that we never discussed any of her feelings! That was why our "communication" did not work. We could have used all the techniques known to man, but as long as the agenda was directed toward expressing blame for causing the feelings instead of communicating the feelings themselves, the conversation was destined to go nowhere.

Our exchanges failed because we shifted off topic. What we needed to focus on—our feelings or our needs—was replaced by a new subject: who did what to whom. Instead of sharing about our frustration, pain, and anger, the topic became: "Who was the good guy and who was the bad guy?" Rather than talking about the *problem*, we fought about *who caused it.* Our battle over blame shifted our discussion from what was wrong to who was wrong.

Three Types of Conversations

There is a difference between *having problems* communicating and *failing* to communicate. Two people who speak different languages will have problems communicating. Without a common tongue, it is virtually impossible to talk about thoughts, needs, or feelings—and, as you can easily see, that is a problem.

Failing to communicate is a different matter all together. If two people are not able to have a successful conversation (meaning that there is a successful negotiation in which each party gets what he/she wants), we call that a communication problem. In my opinion, *this term is not accurate.*

Most couples do not have a *problem* communicating. They are speaking the same language. Their struggles occur because they *fail* to communicate. They are unable to express their idea—or to get their partner to listen—because they do not follow the rules of proper communication.

The reason this distinction is so important is because it emphasizes responsibility. To say that "there is a *problem* with our communication" is like saying, "I am not well," or observing, "The relationship is not healthy." These statements do not emphasize ownership or accountability. To emphasize that a couple is *failing* to communicate more accurately represents what is happening, and that places the responsibility for an unsuccessful conversation on the person talking.

To better understand this distinction we need to understand that not all conversations are forms of communication. There are three types of conversations people have with one another.

1. Communicating
2. Correcting
3. Combating

Each type of conversation has a different objective. Communication is only one type of discussion. The other two types of conversation, correcting and combating, involve verbal exchanges, but the interactions resulting from each are distinctly dissimilar and have little relationship to true communication.

When we share our lives, our dreams, or our feelings we are engaging in true communication. *Communication* lets another person know who we are and provides an opportunity to connect.

When our verbal exchanges seek to get us what we want by altering something about the other person—behavior, attitude, etc.—we are no longer communicating, we are *correcting*. Once the focus moves to modifying the other person by emphasizing what we see as the mistakes that the other person has made or behaviors that have hurt or frustrated us, the direction of the discussion shifts off ourselves and on to him or her. When we accentuate our partner's deficiencies rather than simply expressing what we desire, we are no longer sharing ourselves. Rather, we are "fixing" our spouse. In the correction mode, the topic centers on what our mate has or has not done and does not address our real needs explicitly.

As the discussion becomes agitated, couples often move into a *combative* mode. The phrase "an eye for an eye" comes from the tendency to instinctively wish to hurt those who have hurt us. That sentiment also underlies the essence of a combative conversation.

There are moments when couples say things that they may not mean, but they say them anyway, with the intention of hurting the other person. The motive does not come from a place of malice. It is just an attempt to make the other person experience our pain.

The changing focus & goals of our discussions

	Focus	Goal of Discussion
Communicating	Sharing	To Be Heard
Correcting	Correcting	Change
Combating	Hurting	Remorse

Each style of conversing has its own focus, and objective. There are three different directions and destinations to our dialogues, and consequently we see these three distinct types of conversations: communicating, correcting, and combating.

Communicating

"Hey, I went and saw my Aunt Karen today. She is doing much better."

"You would not believe the kind of day that I had ..."

29

"I was disappointed that the car was left outside in the rain after it just got washed."

These are examples of real communication. One person in the relationship is letting the other person know what is going on . . . without any demands or hidden agendas.

True communication is the sharing of personal information, with the only expectation being that we will be heard. We can talk about needs, feelings, thoughts, desires, and dreams—as long as the topic centers on ourselves.

When you are really communicating you can discuss anything, but you must be sure that your intent and motives are pure, meaning that you are filling the other person in on what is going on in your life, nothing more.

Exercise - What I Appreciate And What I Resent

This is one of my favorite exercises for promoting communication. Sit down with each other and alternate back and forth sharing *one* thing you appreciate, and *one* thing you resent about the other person. The exchange needs to go on until both parties have exhausted their list of appreciations and resentments. It usually takes at least ten rounds, about 30 to 35 minutes.

There are three guidelines that keep the conversation moving in a positive direction: no take backs, no tag backs, and/or no feedback.

First, be careful not to negate your appreciation with your resentment. "I like how you help with the kitchen, but I get frustrated when you do not sweep the floor." That was a take back. The praise was erased by the criticism. Shuffle the two around so the issue of not sweeping is shared with something unrelated like how you appreciate the way he/she deals with the kids.

The second suggestion is avoid tag backs, or rebutting your partner's resentment with your own. Your spouse may comment how he resents you for not accepting his family. Then in your next round you share how you resent your spouse for listening to his family over you. It is fair to bring that up at some point during the exercise, but it should not be on the heels of your partner's remarks.

Third, there is no discussion about any of these items, or no feedback. Everything that is shared is simply heard at face value. You may request clarification about what was meant or said, but you cannot demand proof or examples of when that has occurred. All the comments need to be kept short and to the point. Elaborate details should be left out, and if the other person needs additional explanation it will be up to the listener to request it.

Stay within the structure of the exercise by starting each comment with the appropriate phrase. "What I appreciate about you is... and what I resent about you is..."

Using the word "and" is important to make both statements of equal value. The word "but", used between the two statements, negates what you appreciate, and emphasizes your resentment.

Give the exercise a spin. Hook up with your spouse or significant other and experience what it is like to truly communicate.

Two Rules Of Engagement

The exercise above is very effective, both because it forces both participants to simply share what is going on and because there is no allowance for discussion or debate about any of the topics. The goal of a healthy conversation is to share our feelings, thoughts, and needs and to have the other person hear us. Real communication offers up who we are—with no additional expectations or demands.

It would be wonderful if the other person were to change as a result of our conversation. And, in fact, this is often what happens. For example, because we are open and communicating, our spouse will respond in kind. However, remember that if we enter the discussion with the agenda of altering our partner's behavior, by trying to get him or her to say something specific, like to admit guilt. Then we are not communicating, we are correcting.

Correcting

To express ourselves and to have our partner listen should be the focus and goal of any discussion, but that is not always what happens. Our conversations frequently develop alternative, short-term objectives that shift us away from communicating and into correcting.

When we are hurt, the direction of our discussion may become diverted. The topic can quickly shift to averting our partner's hurtful words or actions and thus to stopping our pain. This may sound like a reasonable course, but it completely transforms the conversation.

~

Susan comes into their home office and begins firing at Keith. "As soon as you get home, you go right to the computer. Why can't you spend a few minutes with the family?"

~

Although it may appear that Susan is expressing her feeling of frustration regarding the computer, what is really going on is that she is attempting to amend Keith's behavior. The focus of the conversation is on Keith, not on herself. The direction the dialogue takes (and its focus) defines the conversation as one of correction rather than communication.

How could this exchange become a communication rather than a correction? Susan might say, "I feel sad when you come home and immediately sit down at the computer. It makes me think you don't want to spend time with the family." The topic has changed from looking at the other person to addressing one's self. It is now an example of *true communication*.

The difference between the comment "Why can't you spend time?" and "It makes me feel like you don't want to spend time," is that the first is an *attack* and the second is a *statement*. In the first example, Susan is focused on changing Keith, while in the second, Susan is sharing information about herself.

Correcting ultimately fails as a form of communication because it casts blame. To say that someone needs to load the dishwasher differently implies that the other person has done it wrong (and you do it right!). By approaching the conversation in this way we are not sharing, we are telling the other person what to do or not do, say or not say, think or not think—and even feel or not feel.

Talking about our feelings of hurt, sadness, disappointment, or betrayal is left out of this "correcting" conversation. Why? Perhaps it is because we think that to reveal these feelings might make us too vulnerable. Anger, irritation, annoyance or frustration may be mentioned briefly, but reference to our emotions is generally absent or not emphasized. When a conversation is occurring in a corrective mode there is no openness or softness. As a result, by the end of the conversation there is no feeling of intimacy or closeness.

Not only does the focus change when we correct, but so does the goal—*what we want to hear back from our mate*. To have our partner listen attentively is no longer enough. Once we have shifted into correcting, our agenda is focused on getting our spouse to accept responsibility and to admit what he/she did was wrong.

Remarks like "It sounds like your day with the kids was difficult," or "It's great your meeting went so well," are not adequate responses. In the correction mode, what we need is an admission of guilt.

Years ago, there was a program on TV called "Mad About You." In one scene, Helen Hunt, the main female character, was fighting with Paul Riser, the male lead. Riser had just proven his point and was now standing with hands on hips, staring at Helen, waiting for her to respond. She looked at him for a while before finally confessing, "I was wrong."

Paul was not satisfied, "And more importantly?"

Then Helen replies again. "And you were right."

Paul Riser, who was also the creator of the program, nailed it dead-on. Those two phrases—"You were right" and "I was wrong"—are the only words that will end a conversation when it is in a corrective mode. When we are correcting, we are waiting to hear some variation on this theme. The dialogue may stop, but the issue remains alive for years, until we hear our spouse admit their mistakes and/or acknowledge our position.

This shift in goal and focus makes all of our conventionally accepted "communication techniques" fail. Using "I" messages or active listening techniques will not work as long as the agenda, whether stated or implied, is really to change the other person's behavior or attitude in some way. When one partner is operating in the corrective mode, all the other hears is that he or she is wrong and that the complainer is right. Hiding the message in some "communication exercise" only makes the other person feel manipulated. Using "I" messages may perhaps lessen the other person's defensiveness, creating the possibility that he/she will listen. However, if the conversation is being conducted in a corrective mode, the speaker is not going to feel satisfied with simply being heard—that would not be enough; the speaker will need to hear the other person admit that he/she was wrong, maybe even to say that, whatever the issue may be, it will not happen again. Even though the technique seemingly "worked" (it got the message across), it probably did not satisfy the needs of the speaker and therefore will be perceived as a communication failure.

Combating

The focus of the *Combative* mode of discussion is not on sharing feelings or on pointing out problems; it is about inflicting pain. When any human being feels hurt, the first, virtually instinctive, impulse is to hurt back—and this is the essence of a combative conversation. Often, things are said that are not really meant. That is because the objective here is not expressive, but experiential: to make the other person feel the level of pain that we feel. Once the direction of our discussion changes so does our goal. "I hear you" or "You're right, I'm wrong" is not going to be enough to stop the conflict. When the conversation becomes combative, even an admission of guilt is not sufficient. The speaker wants to see real remorse. The confrontation will continue until the other person shows some kind of deep regret—like this.

~

Ken came in and asked about Joyce's day. "How was your afternoon with the twins?"

"It was nice. We went to the mall and then stopped at Sally's to get the boys to play together." Joyce was pleased to hear Ken's interest in the family.

"Did you go to lunch anywhere?" Ken probed for more details.

Joyce continued to respond positively. "Yeah, I got the boys some take-out meals and they ate as we came back from the park."

Ken then pounced. "I noticed! There was trash and fries all over the car. How many times have I asked you not to use the car as a dining room?"

Angry at Ken's sudden criticism, Joyce fired back. "What should I do, ground the boys because they made a mess? They're toddlers."

"What if you didn't let them eat in the car? Is that too hard a concept?" Now Ken is even angrier because Joyce was not taking responsibility for the messy condition of the car.

Joyce came back at him. "If you weren't at work so much, I could get some help with the twins. I don't know why you are on me about how I parent when you're never around!"

Ken then took another shot. "It's not your parenting, it is your housekeeping that disgusts me. The reason I'm not around is because this place is a pigsty."

~

Look at that progression—or *regression*! Both Ken and Joyce started off communicating. For Ken, the conversation did not go anywhere because he already had a different agenda. Instead of sharing his frustration, he began to correct Joyce. After Joyce began pointing out Ken's shortcomings, the argument escalated to the combative state, and that is when Ken went for the jugular.

The shift in the direction of our conversations is problematic enough, but there is also a change in our goals that makes resolution impossible.

The problem is not that our discussions focus on difficult issues. The trouble is that what we expect back from the other person is increasingly impossible for him/her to give. We not only want our spouse to hear how he/she is responsible for our pain and admit his/her mistake, but in order to have closure our spouse must feel as bad as we do. Listening to us talk about our upset does not end the discussion. Once we have escalated into the combative mode we need him/her to feel our pain, as well.

What's Wrong?

What is wrong, as we have already seen, is that many such conversations are focused on who is wrong rather than on the facts of the situation, that one person seems bent on making the partner the problem. Instead of communicating directly about an upset, the complainer is correcting the other person. Changing a few phrases, or being kinder and gentler about how we say things, would not generally make a difference because as long as we are focused on changing our spouse we are not going to be sharing about ourselves.

Making these distinctions between the three various styles of conversation can help couples to recognize what they are doing wrong as we seek effective communication. It is also vital in identifying how to make things right. However, knowledge alone is not sufficient. The problem with blame extends beyond verbal dialogues. The difficulties that couples experience with their conversations go deeper than how they speak to each other. Right Fights also prevent them from establishing any kind of connection.

Homework: In order to recognize the different styles, we need to become more familiar with how dissimilar each style feels. Take a few disagreements and role play in your head, or on paper, how it would sound as the focus of the discussion changes.

Start with the combative model. Think about how you could express yourself when the outcome you want is to hurt your partner, as he/she has hurt you. Think of how you could articulate your pain in such a way that would make your spouse feel guilty, sad, or depressed. Include in your role-play what your partner would say.

Then play out the same situation with the goal of wanting him/her to change, the corrective conversation. Script what responses you would want to hear; "you were right" or "I will never do that again." Finally, try real communication. What would you say if you were to merely share information? And what might the response be if you simply asked your partner to listen?

Chapter 4

Love-Based Solutions^{SM}

We are taking the wrong approach

Homework

On her way home, Jill called to find out if the kids had completed their homework. Rick answered, "I just checked with both Daniel and Faith and it's all done."

When she walked in the door, Rick was watching the news while the kids were playing in Faith's room. Jill asked to see their work and quickly discovered that neither child has done the homework. Jill was upset. Part of her frustration was with the kids, but it was also with Rick. There he was, sitting on the sofa taking care of his needs, and she was barely going to be able to change her clothes before having to sit down with Daniel and Faith.

As a result of her irritation, Rick found a bit of a chill in the air when he tried to talk with his wife. He had no idea why she was in this mood. His response was to steer clear and give her some space. His behavior only confirmed Jill's belief that Rick did not care about her feelings.

Later that evening, when Rick asked Jill what was bothering her, things exploded. "I specifically called to ask, and you said it was all handled. But it wasn't. I had to do everything, and, once again, I didn't have time to take care of my needs." Jill blurted out her frustration.

"Well, I don't appreciate you coming home and giving me the silent treatment. I asked them, and they both said it was done," Rick retorted.

Recognizing that the conversation was going nowhere, Rick summarized his response with, "Whatever!" and he walked away.

If you were to ask Jill and Rick what went wrong, the response would probably be, "We just can't communicate." Actually, their verbiage—the choice of words they used with each other—was adequate. Jill and Rick both used "I" messages and shared their upset with one another without attacking or blaming. *What went wrong was that Jill and Rick both went into a protective stance.*

Jill's high emotional charge sabotaged the conversation. Jill was detached and disconnected when she shared her pain. Feeling her distance, Rick focused his irritation at her withdrawal and was unsupportive of her frustration. As a result, the topic became who was right and who was wrong.

What if, instead of worrying about how or what was said, we address Jill's mood. The words we use are a reflection of the way we feel. Consequently, if we want to change the way people speak to each other, the most direct route would be to change how they feel about one another.

Imagine if this same situation should arise and the two of them remain in a close, affectionate, loving state of mind. Would decreasing their esthetic distance change their dialogue? Here is the new scenario:

Greeting Rick with a hug and a kiss, Jill asks, "So, how was your day?"

Rick responds in kind, "Fine, how was yours?"

Jill then replies, "It was nice, but I was a little frustrated when I came home and found that neither Daniel nor Faith had done their homework."

Rick's response comes in the same soft tone as Jill's. "Oh, both of them told me they were finished. Do you need me to go work with them?"

"No, I took care of it. I simply wanted to let you know, because it left me feeling irritated." Jill again emphasizes her feelings.

Rick replies, "I can imagine. Next time I'll make sure the kids actually show me their work."

The situation has now become a non-event, not because of some dramatic shift in how they communicated, but because Jill stayed soft and connected. In this scenario, Jill expresses her frustration and Rick hears it. Why? Because Jill remains close. She does not let her feelings of frustration drive her into a defensive space.

Our words are not the problem. It is our emotions and, more specifically, how we respond to our feelings that hamper our communication. Couples can play with the language they use, but if their emotional state is not conducive to loving conversation, then it will be the same fight on a different day.

Instead of droning on about how couples need to talk "nicer," I want to propose a different, unique answer to our conflicts. What I am about to suggest here—and throughout the rest of the book—is that *if a couple wants to improve their interaction, they will need to learn to speak "in love".*

How We See That the Problem Is a Problem

Albert Einstein once said, "How we form our questions determines our answers." To see the solution to our disagreements, we need to change the way in which we are looking at the problem.

If one of my children were having difficulties at school, my mind would form ideas about "why." Based on my knowledge or beliefs about my child and the situation, I would draw some conclusions and create an action plan.

If I believed that my child was lazy, I might be asking myself, "How can I push this child to get his work done?"

But what if my assumption was incorrect? Then, not only would the question be wrong, but all of my solutions would be off, as well. For instance, what if the child was having trouble with his vision but had not been diagnosed as such?

How we see a problem can sometimes *be* the problem.

To discover new solutions, we need to change how we think about the issues. First, let us examine how couples conceptualize the struggles in their marriages.

Most people believe that their conflicts create pain and that the wounds we carry produce distance. Based on this assumption, couples tend to work toward improving their communication in the hope that if there are no conflicts, there will be no pain and the two will grow closer.

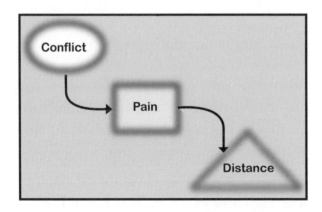

Eighty percent of couples seeking marital counseling believe that communicating is their biggest problem. This statistic reflects the notion that feelings of lovelessness stem from an inability to communicate effectively. The distance in the relationship is seen as more symptomatic rather than problematic, meaning that a loss of intimacy is thought to be the result of a failure to negotiate or a refusal to share by one or both parties.

What if it is actually the other way around? What if it is the distance we create between us that prevents us from communicating? What if the cycle starts with pain, which creates distance, and finally ends with difficult conversations?

It is true that our pain is sometimes stimulated by something our spouse says. At other times, though, our upset is the result of something that he/she does or does not do, like leaving the toilet seat up. Moreover, there are times when it might be what was *not* said (for instance, "I love you" or "How was your day?") that hurts us. It is not always the other person's words that cause pain. We are sometimes just as hurt by their silences.

Conflicts occur after we have been hurt. Our communications are an attempt to resolve our feelings. It is true that our disagreements can create further pain, but most of the time something had happened to prompt the conversation in the first place.

Our struggles start with pain. Once we are wounded, that feeling quickly escalates into the belief that we were wronged, and the fact that it is our intimate partner who has caused us emotional pain makes it feel very personal. If a stranger were to blurt out a rude remark we would probably ignore or dismiss the incident, but we expect our intimates to use caution, to be sensitive. Hence, when our mate hurts us it cuts to the quick.

As soon as we begin feeling slighted, our instincts kick in and we create space, either by pushing away or by pulling back. It is as normal as recoiling from a hot stove. When we are hurt, we distance ourselves from the source of our pain.

No one *intends* to get into a Right Fight. We merely want to right the wrong we have suffered. In an effort to correct the problem, we end up correcting our partner. It is easier and safer to address the person who hurt us than to make ourselves vulnerable and expose our wounds.

Consequently, the conversation centers on who is wrong instead of on what is wrong.

Our next move, generally, is to wait and watch, hoping to see whether our "communication" brings about any changes. When the conversation only produces a negative reaction, we again feel wounded, the wound turns into a feeling of being wronged, and we withdraw. Whatever we "communicate" from this point on is likely to come out sounding like a correction, which causes our partner to be more defensive. The cycle continues on and on. It becomes the fight that never ends.

The Fight That Never Ends

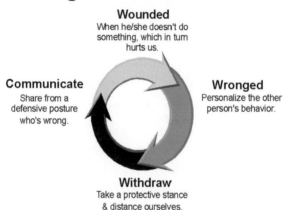

Wounded
When he/she doesn't do something, which in turn hurts us.

Communicate
Share from a defensive posture who's wrong.

Wronged
Personalize the other person's behavior.

Withdraw
Take a protective stance & distance ourselves.

The other option is to say nothing and simply withdraw. We could choose to sit quietly, waiting for a response, waiting for the other party to recognize our pain and to right the wrong. Of course, when no gesture is made we will again feel hurt and unimportant and the cycle will continue without a word said.

Communication comes toward the end of the process. Our partner's response can increase or diminish our upset, but the dialogue does not initiate the process. Our "communication" does not create our pain. It is *our pain* that creates our conflicts. It is our wounds, not our words, that are the problem, and it is love, not language, that will be the solution.

The Problem Is a Shift in Our Upset

The problem with most relationships is physiological, not psychological. Our emotions, the feelings of hurt, sorrow, and fear, place couples in a protective place, and in turn removes them from a connective space. What we say or how we say it can aid in promoting or preventing communication, but it is the level of their upset that will set the tone for any conversation.

There is yet another key difference among the three types of conversations described in the last chapter. Each type—*communicative, corrective and combative*—has its own focal point and objective, but our level of emotional upset also shifts the conversation from communicating to correcting and, finally, to combating.

If we were to rate the intensity of our emotional charge from zero to ten, we would see that couples that are *communicating* are carrying a "charge" of between zero and three. As the level of upset climbs and reaches the range of four to seven, couples begin *correcting* one another. When the upset is at its worst—between eight and ten—things become *combative*.

Once our emotional upset has gone above three or four on a scale of ten, it is impossible to have a "normal" communication. Once one participant has allowed intense feelings to produce a guarded stance, he or she may withdraw. Feeling our disconnection, the other person is going to be inclined to pull away, as well. What we say or how we say it is irrelevant. When our significant other notices that we have "donned our armor" and "drawn our sword," he or she will do the same.

As the tension, hurt, and frustration builds between two people, their conversation degenerates quickly into a corrective or combative mode. When couples are carrying a high emotional charge from all the old, unresolved issues, their "armor" may become semi-permanent as it rusts on.

The relatively orderly downward spiral from communicating to correcting and, finally, to combating is most frequently seen in newer, young relationships. Sad to say, after years of marriage, many couples more commonly move directly into a combative mode. This almost-instant high-energy emotional charge causes a "communication" on even the smallest of issues to erupt, at times, into a major clash. Comments about simple issues—like a dish being broken, or what time the kids need to be picked up—can flare into huge blowouts.

Emotions begin and sustain our disagreements. To better understand how and why our feelings function as they do, let us spend some time looking at the how our feelings serve us—and how they do not.

Feelings Have Two Functions

Take a moment to list on a piece of paper as many different emotions as you can. It does not matter if you group similar feelings together or free-associate and list them randomly. After writing them down, count them. You will most likely identify between 50 and 150 various emotions.

Now go through your list with two different colored highlighters. With one color, mark all the feelings you see that draw people closer to one another. With the other color, highlight the ones that drive people apart.

You will see that feelings serve one of two functions. They either protect or they connect. All our feelings can be placed in one of two categories. Love, hate, hurt, sorrow, joy, peace, happiness, anger, jealousy, fear, frustration, contentment, excitement—all our emotions are either connecting us or protecting us. When we go back over the list, what we see is that these emotions either open us up or close us down.

Human nature is such that we want to spend time with those people and objects that stimulate pleasant feelings. By contrast, we avoid and want to get away from those people and objects that make us feel bad or promote negative emotions.

Note that these two functions—attraction and repulsion—are mutually exclusive. If a dog is growling, I am not likely to try to pet it.

In the same way, my first response to being hurt by my partner will not be to reach out and give him/her a kiss.

The barriers that protect us are destroying our relationships. This shift from connect to protecting is what creates our Right Fights. The switch from what is wrong to who is wrong is, in fact, the direct result of our protective posture.

Information is power. Therefore, sharing our fears, hurt, or insecurities makes us vulnerable, and gives our partner the "upper hand." Talking about what is wrong causes us to feel unprotected. We want to share our hurt, but we fear that exposing our pain will provide an opportunity for our partner to inflict more.

It is no vulnerability in talking about *their* behavior, pointing out *their* mistakes, and "communicating" about *their* missteps. When the conversation is directed toward our partner, we feel less exposed than when discussing our own miscues. Addressing the problems in our partner is a much stronger and safer topic than sharing our pain.

Unfortunately, these corrections of our partner's behavior are seen as an attack and stimulate our partner to go into a protective place. A negative feedback loop is then created. Angry about something said, we naturally push our spouse away, which angers our mate, who then pushes back. Of course, now I am even angrier that my spouse is pushing me, so I shove even harder. Around and around the battle goes, where it stops nobody knows.

What we want is understanding, support and closeness. What is produced by our self-protective space is distance and disagreements. In order to create the changes we desire, we need to recognize that it is our feelings that are at fault. Simply changing what we say is not as important or effective as becoming responsible for how we feel, think, and respond to our spouse.

The Problem Is . . .

❖ the people we love hurt us

❖ when we are hurt by the people we love we feel unloved

❖ when we feel unloved we withdraw our love

❖ when our partner feels our withdrawal he or she feels hurt, unloved and, in turn, withdraws; and

❖ when our partner withdraws his or her love we again feel hurt and unloved, and we retreat further.

The reason so many marriages are in trouble is that love and hurt go hand and hand. The more we love someone, the more sensitive we are to being wounded by a comment, a gesture, or a glance. The only way to immunize ourselves from pain is to immunize ourselves from love. That is exactly where the problem lies.

The problem is not that we become hurt but that when we feel hurt we protect ourselves from pain by withdrawing our love. *We then make our mate responsible for fixing the problem* by asking him/her to love us.

You cannot hug a porcupine. Our partner does not respond to our recoil by running after us. Hurt by our withholding, our intimate partner believes he/she is not loved, and then he/she denies us love. This standoff is where most marriages are stuck. Each party is waiting for the other to admit their mistake and take a step forward.

The Practice of Psychotherapy vs. The Practice of Love

Alcoholics Anonymous defines insanity as doing the same thing and expecting different results. Given the research conclusion that only about 15% of couples benefit long term from counseling, it seems quite clear that to continue doing therapy as we have is, in some sense, a form of insanity.

The majority of psychotherapists focus on how couples communicate[vii], but, as we have seen, that is not the problem. Other approaches address a couple's negative beliefs that one or the other was wronged, unloved, or betrayed. Therapy, at times, addresses the differences between men and women by delving into their childhoods. However, all of these various therapeutic styles share one fatal flaw. Despite the dozen or more tactics in marital therapy, every style has the same underlying orientation and, therefore, makes the same mistake. Each seeks to change a couple's thoughts and/or feelings in order to restore their sense of connection. It is a "Field of Dreams" approach to love and marriage.

In the movie "The Field of Dreams," Actor Kevin Costner plays a corn farmer who hears a voice telling him, "If you build it, he will come!" He proceeds to cut down his field and to build a baseball diamond. Then ghosts from the classic age of baseball begin to appear and play ball.

Virtually every school of psychology believes that "if you fix it, love will come." The "it", changes, depending on each school's orientation. If you change a couple's communication—or understand gender differences—or deal with their childhood issues—then love will return. The advocates' hypothesis is that by addressing one of these problem areas the marriage will be renewed.

Couples need to relate
in order to communicate.

Maybe the issue is not that complicated. We propose that the primary problem is that couples have been hurt and now stand off. It is their protective response that is preventing their communication as well as their ability to reconnect.

As the nursery rhyme goes, "First comes love, then comes marriage…" Love is what creates our relationship, and only love can make our marriage work. When a couple is in a connected space, the two people in the relationship can talk openly and honestly about their wounds, hurts, and disappointments, and the conversation will bring them closer.

The process of re-directing our relationships to the experience of love is the hallmark of what I have termed, "the practice of love." This work is not centered on psychological principles. Rather, it is built around the understanding and practice of love. Love is the means, not the goal. Coming to an issue or problem already connected is the only way to approach your differences.

What Is The Solution?

The opposite of blame is responsibility. If even one person in the relationship takes responsibility for his/her withdrawal, the two will connect, and at that point communication can—and will—occur. As long as a couple stays joined in love, or *practices love*, they can talk about *what is wrong* without being pulled into the battles over *who is wrong*.

The fact that we sometimes hurt each other is not going to change. What needs to change is that each of us must be responsible for our own recoil. We need to remain in love. By confessing our hurt in a mood of love, our partner can hear us and respond in love. We do not have to "fix" all our problems to restore our marriage. The fact that we have stopped loving has created our problems, so once we learn to love again we can and will communicate our needs, work out our differences, and have the closeness we have been seeking all along. Love heals all wounds.

The only question that remains is: *what is love?* Love is the theme of every mushy song on the radio. It is the sappy sentiment of many greeting cards. So what is it? No one really knows what love is or how to create it.

Homework: Make a connection prior to sharing your feelings. Your homework is to think of something that you want to discuss with your partner. Pick a topic with a "moderate" to "mild" emotional charge. Then, before you say anything, take some time to make a connection. Do whatever you two do to "hook up"—spend time together, go out on a date, or have sex—then share what is on your mind.

Notice whether or not it is easier for you to express yourself. Note if it is it easier for your partner to hear you.

Section Two

REFOCUSING
On What's Right

Chapter 5

What Is Love?

Understanding love and attention

The Vow Was to Love

Because I was raised in a single-parent home, my weekends were not always filled with fun family time. The fact that my father was a minister made it even worse. I was dragged to more weddings than I care to remember. By the age of ten I could recite the traditional wedding vows by heart . . . "Do you, *So and So*, take *So and So* to be your lawfully wedded wife and promise to be her loving and faithful husband, for richer or for poorer, in joy and in sorrow, in sickness and in health, for as long as you both shall live?" Even though I could say it backwards and forwards, I never really understood what it meant. Not until my own marriage started falling apart.

I would love to report that my marriage was perfect, but after reading about some of the conflicts between my wife and me you are surely aware that it was not. We had some good times, but there also had been very dark periods. At one point, I was leading a divorce recovery workshop, and from one week to the next I was not sure if I was going to facilitate or be a participant.

Our troubles peaked when, after some eight years of marriage, I came to the realization that my feeling of affection for my spouse had all but disappeared. I cared about her and thought of her as a wonderful parent, but my own feelings of attraction had died out.

Without the bond that had originally brought us together, I found myself short with her. The cute little things that brought us together had become the petty irritations that widened the gap between us. We seemed to have no tolerance for each other's differences. With no connection there was no concern about spending time together, so there was nothing to counteract our growing disconnection.

In hindsight, I can see the reason the marriage was failing was that we did not understand our vows. As a child, I had thought that those vows were a commitment to stay together. No matter what our financial status, feelings or health, the commitment was to remain a couple. Yet, as the years passed with Lynda, I realized that being married had become more like being roommates. Although we were dedicated to remaining a couple, that did not make us married. Those difficult and dark years finished off my childish views of marriage as a simple pledge to stay.

The real meaning of marriage is expressed in our covenant to love. I had promised to be *"her loving and faithful husband."* The commitment was to devote myself to her. No matter what happened in our lives, the vow was to love.

Neither Lynda nor I really understood what that meant. Consequently, we both failed to fulfill our pledge. As a result, our marriage was failing. We did not recognize that without love there is no marriage.

What Is Love?

Ask a hundred people to define love and you will get a hundred different answers. "Love is patient." "Love is kind." "Love is that warm feeling inside." However, when we look closely at their words, they are just as vague as love itself.

People describe love as an actions or a feeling. Some say love is "a kind word," for example, while others experience love as an energy or excitement. Neither illustration, however, serves as a practical, working definition.

Exercise-Create Your Own Definition of Love

Take out a pad of post-it notes and write out what you think love is, using one sheet for each of your individual descriptions.

Using the phrases quoted earlier, for example, I would write on one sheet, "love is patient," and then on another, "love is kind," and so on. Once you have written out every possible way of defining love, go through your pile of notes and sort them by similar characteristics. One group will be a feeling pile. The other will be an action pile.

What we see in this exercise is that our definitions are just descriptions. What you will find is that all of your sheets of paper will divide very nicely into one or the other of these two categories. They are behavioral or emotional representations of what we associate with the word love. Yet, they do not capture a useful definition.

This is not to say there is something wrong with our own descriptions of love, but it does show that our descriptions are very subjective. If you are thinking of love as an action and your partner is looking for a feeling, both of you will be hurt and frustrated. One person may see himself/herself as being loving, while the other person does not. One way is not better than another; in fact, each has its own problems and each has its shortcomings.

Love Is a Feeling . . .

The dictionary defines love as "affection felt between two people." If love is a feeling—*affection*—then what does it mean when one of you is feeling angry, irritated, sad, or disappointed? Does that indicate an absence of love? And if you are upset with your partner, how do you go about feeling those feelings of affection once again? How can you love when you are not feeling affectionate? When you are feeling hurt or angry with your partner, how do you shift those emotions with feelings of fondness?

There is no clear definition of love.

The difficulty with defining love as a feeling is that most people cannot experience negative and positive emotions simultaneously. Our emotions tend to be black or white, in that we are either feeling self-protective (negative) or connective (positive) emotions. Anger and other such harsh emotions, for instance, prevent us from also experiencing compassion. It is difficult to feel injured by someone and at the same time to feel the more tender emotion of caring for that same person; the feelings that connect us or protect us are mutually exclusive.

However, we can—and probably have—felt annoyed and disappointed in the same moment, because both are in the same negative, self-protective family of feelings. It is not so simple to feel affectionate, though, when we are also feeling abused.

To successfully communicate our hurt, sorrow or anger, we must share it "in love." That means that love needs to be expressed or somehow transmitted to our partners in conjunction with, and at the same moment as, our sense of hurt, sorrow, and anger. However, if love is a feeling, then how can this be done?

To be fully committed to love would preclude us from expressing negative emotions. But how can one feel warm and fuzzy while feeling hot and angry? One simply cannot . . . and that is the problem.

It is as though our hearts are equipped with only one arm to hold our emotions. Either we embrace our love and forget our pain or we express our hurt and risk losing sight of love.

Depending solely upon emotions to define love would also place us in a passive position. Although we might understand the feeling(s) of love, we would not know how to turn those feelings into actions, either for ourselves or for others. Our emotional descriptions of love simply do not give us the power to create or communicate love, especially when we are not feeling loved.

To talk about love purely as an emotion may also leave us powerless to renew the relationship, because most of us believe that we have no control over our emotions—they just happen. While we certainly can recognize when a feeling is present and when it is not, we are seldom, if ever, consciously aware of how the feeling came to be, how it was generated. It is as though feelings force us to be reactive, never pro-active. So, if we are incapable of manufacturing an emotion, our commitments can become flimsy. Describing love solely as an emotion, then, implies that a couple will only stay together as long as the "good" feelings continue. Once the bond between them is gone, so is the basis for their relationship.

Love Is an Action . . .

What is the problem with defining love as some kind act? The difficulty arises because our unique experiences create incompatible definitions. Not everyone sees loving actions in the same way, since none of us shares identical life events. Because couples do not share a common point of reference—at least in the beginning of a relationship—the actions that one partner may think of as loving may not be considered so by the other. These mismatched interpretations of loving action can create the perception, conscious or unconscious, that we are not loved. Bob and Jan provide a great example.

~

When Bob was growing up, to slap another person lightly on the behind was a common expression of affection in his family. In a way, it was a tender game of tag. Bob remembers his father playfully chasing him up the stairs, trying to give him a rap on the rear, as Bob squealed with laughter.

When Bob married Jan, he began incorporating this playful gesture into his expression of affection for her. However, her response was not what he expected. As soon as he slapped her on the backside, the fun came to a grinding halt and Jan's mood unexpectedly became cold and grim. For years, Bob and Jan did not understand how things could be going so well and then, suddenly, fall apart. These brief encounters incited many of their Right Fights. Bob saw Jan as frigid, cutting him off every time he became lighthearted. To Jan, Bob was the one with the problem. Jan's take on the whole situation was that it was Bob who unexpectedly became angry. From her point of view, it was Bob who was killing their playfulness.

After going to therapy, they discovered that in Jan's family, roughhousing was never allowed. When things started to get a little too rambunctious, her Dad would swat Jan lightly on the behind as a signal for her to knock it off. Bob and Jan had markedly different associations with this simple pat. To Bob it was an expression of affection, but for Jan it meant she had done something wrong. Bob's affection was felt by Jan as rejection. Their differing view of what it was to love kept them from feeling loved.

~

Seeing love as action is more definable, yet it, too, is very subjective. Doing what seems loving to us may not be felt as loving by our partner. Here is a very personal example.

When I feel stressed, my response is to want to be left alone to process or re-energize myself—for me it is an "inside job." Lynda, on the other hand, relieves her stress by talking about it, by sharing it with someone else.

Given those criteria for dealing with stress, when Lynda is having a bad (stressful) day, I—as a gesture of love—tend to want to give my partner some space. But if I do that, she—instead of feeling loved—may feel rejected or abandoned. Remember, what she really wants is to sit and talk.

The situation could also be reversed and have the same disastrous result. Lynda, noticing that I am having a hard time, may instinctively want to get me to talk about it, but the harder she pushes me to share, the more frustrated and badgered I feel, and when I refuse what she sees as her "help," she interprets my action as a personal rejection—she feels pushed away.

Because couples usually see their partners as extensions of themselves, they are likely to evaluate the other person's needs based on what they themselves need. When our love and support of the other person is rejected, because it is not what he/she wants, but what we would want, we feel unloved. From our point of self-reference, there seems to be no other interpretation. When our partner refuses our help, he/she is rejecting us. By stepping back from that limited point of view, we can begin to see rejection is not the issue. The problem is that we do not see our partner through his or her eyes, but through our own. As a result, we are not giving what our partner wants and needs, but what we want.

Love Is Attention

Love is not limited to a feeling, or even to a group of feelings, although *love is felt emotionally*. Love is not any particular act or a series of behaviors, although *love is expressed through our actions*. Love encompasses our sentiments and our deeds, but *love is something more*.

I came to a personal definition of love when Lynda and I were working our way through that period when we nearly separated and divorced. I found intimacy through two disparate channels, psychotherapy and spirituality. As a psychotherapist and a Christian, I had first-hand knowledge of the power of each calling, but despite a lifetime's worth of knowledge I found myself unable to focus on either power source as it applied to my personal situation. Communication and prayer were in front of me all the time, but I could not see them.

At about the time I was running my divorce recovery groups and simultaneously wondering if I was going to be divorced, Lynda and I undertook a course of formal therapy with a trusted therapist. I was soon amazed to discover that counseling was helping. Amazed? Yes. The source of my amazement was that the therapist was focusing on all of the same topics that Lynda and I had already been discussing at home, and our interactions with the therapist were covering just about the same ground. Nevertheless, even after only a few sessions, our relationship was improving.

Because I am a therapist, I could not help wondering what was at the heart of these changes. Expressing our feelings or asking for our needs to be met was not, and never had been, a big problem for either Lynda or me. Therefore, I was not sure what was making the difference.

At this particular time in my life I was also dissatisfied with my relationship with God. In the same way that I felt no connection with my wife, I was also feeling distant from God. To improve my spiritual life I began to study about prayer and meditation. I was very pleased to find that it almost immediately began to make a huge difference in my life, but I was also puzzled, because I had always prayed. What was different now?

I began looking at other religions that taught meditation. Tibetan Buddhism advocated surrendering oneself by continually giving full attention to God. "Attention is the root of the mind." By continually surrendering our attention to God we are able to transcend all our thoughts and arrive at a place of Divine Bliss.

I began applying this principle to my relationship with my Christian faith. Much to my surprise, I discovered that through bringing my attention to God, I no longer struggled with the musings of my mind; my heart was given over to Him in love. Consequently, my devotional life began to expand. My feelings of inadequacy, guilt, and self-doubt were seemingly melted away by simply surrendering them to God through the gift of my attention.

As I practiced this incredibly simple act, my heart welled up with a powerful sense of peace and love. I became certain that there was a direct correlation—I began to see that love and attention were, ultimately, the same.

At that point, I recognized that the giving of my attention was also creating and reinforcing the sense of love in my marriage. The time and attention that Lynda and I were required to bring to therapy was proving to be the primary element that re-formed and trans-formed our bond.

Couples counseling naturally focused our attention on each other. And in addition to our 90-minute sessions, there was the hour spent driving to and from the appointment, as well as our time together at dinner afterwards—we made it a practice to do that after every session so we could continue the bonding process in our own way and at our own pace. All that time spent focusing directly and exclusively on our relationship was breathing life back into our marriage.

By bringing my loving attention to Lynda I was fulfilling my vows in the marriage. As a result, she and I could talk about almost anything, and although we did not always agree, we were able to stay connected. Of course, at times, I hurt her feelings and she hurt mine, but it did not knock us for a loop.

The other strange transformation that occurred was that I no longer seemed to care as much about getting Lynda to agree with me, nor was I as concerned about her doing everything I asked. Feeling my love for her, and her love for me, was, ultimately, all that I wanted. All the other "stuff" was not as important any more.

This simple revelation completely transformed my marriage as well as the way I do marriage counseling.

Once it was obvious that my attention was experienced as love, I began playfully practicing bringing my full attention to my marriage, my clients, and my life. As I did so, not only did I begin to feel more love for my family, but I also felt more love for everyone, all the time, and in every circumstance. I felt more love for my children and my wife than I had experienced in years. Clearly, the hectic nature of my life had stolen my attention from what was most important to me. By consciously bringing my attention back to my family, everything began turning around to where it should have been. Rather than love being the byproduct of something else, love was the answer to my problems.

I discovered that our emptiness had not stemmed from our poor communication or our lack of understanding of each other. The lovelessness we felt at times was not a symptom. It was the problem. Love, through the free gift of our attention, turned out to be the only antidote to the feeling of being unloved.

More than a feeling of warmth or a thought of loyalty—or even an act of kindness—love is the gift of attention. By understanding this, couples can begin to experience their relationship in its "two-armed" form: one arm embracing our pain, the other embracing our partner.

Through the gift of attention, love remains alive even while we express our wounds. And anybody can do it! You can always bring your attention to your spouse no matter what your emotional state. You can be angry and still be attentive to how your partner is feeling. When you give each other your attention, you create a sense of closeness, intimacy, and love regardless of the mood that either you or your partner may be in at that moment.

Homework: Let your partner know how much you love him/her. Do this in any style you would normally express your love. However, do it with as much attention as you can bring to your circumstance.

Notice not only your partner's response to your attentiveness, but also your own internal feelings.

Chapter 6

Measuring, Communicating, And Creating Love

Becoming responsible for love

Date Night

During one particular week, I had worked long hours and, as a result, Lynda and I were a little on edge. It was clear that we needed to reconnect. I made plans with her to go out after work on the following Friday. Unfortunately, my scheme did not go exactly as I hoped. When I got home, Lynda was holding Trevor, our youngest. He had a fever, and she felt she could not leave him with a sitter.

In an instant, I decided, baby-sitter or no baby-sitter, to give her some extra attention to let her know I loved her. I helped take care of Trevor and Wesley, getting them ready for bed. At eight, when the little guys went down, I headed out to the market to pick up her favorite dessert.

While she took care of herself, I put the table together with candles and flowers. I laid out the perfect presentation for her dessert, using our good china and a little background music. This time together was not about me. It was about her. So, it did not matter that it was not some elaborate occasion.

Telling her how much I loved her was almost redundant. All the attention I had brought to the moment made the point. My expression of love and appreciation for her was just icing on the cake. The event filled my heart, as well. In connecting with her, I in turn felt connected.

When we receive attention we know that our partner loves us. When we give it we let the attention-getter know that we love him or her. Just as importantly, when we give attention we arouse feelings of passion within ourselves. Let us examine further and in somewhat greater detail how attention can be used to share, to spur, and to stimulate feelings of affection.

Attention Is How We Measure Love

Imagine that you are sitting in a restaurant, engaging in a bit of people watching. Over in the corner sits a couple completely fixated on each other. They are holding hands, gazing deeply into each other's eyes, totally oblivious to the world around them. Knowing nothing else about them, this much you could predict. If you were to walk over and ask either of them what they were feeling, they would say, "Love." How do you know that? You can see it in the intense, undivided attention they are giving to each other.

Continuing to gaze around the room, you see another couple that is responding very differently to one another than the earlier pair of lovebirds. The woman, leaning forward and speaking animatedly, appears to be desperately trying to get the man's attention. He, however, is more focused on the waitress than on her. After a while, the woman, unable to engage her partner in conversation, sinks dejectedly back into her chair. If you were to stroll over to their table and ask her what she was feeling, you would probably hear her say, "Unloved." How could you predict that? Because intuitively we all understand that love and attention are the same.

The examples of those couples in the restaurant are simple illustrations of how we consciously or unconsciously use attention as a measuring device for love. We gauge how much others love us by the amount of attention they pay to us.

~

Tony walks into the house and mutters a brusque "Hi." There is no eye contact, no touch, and no kiss. He sits down in his favorite chair and picks up *Sports Illustrated*.

Denise may know that Tony loves her, but she does not feel it in his actions. If there has been some tension between them, nothing in his behavior offers any reassurance of his affection.

By contrast, if Tony walks in the door, hugs Denise and asked her how her day was, and then if he lets her know he is going to read for a while, the whole story will be different.

~

Around our house, the relationship between love and attention was confirmed every time the phone rang. The kids would be off playing in the other room, completely contented, until the phone would ring. Then either Wesley or Trevor—sometimes both of them at the same moment—would ask for juice and demand that mommy and daddy play with them. If they could not get a positive response, they would try for negative attention by acting up, fighting, and yelling. As long as Lynda or I were not focusing on anyone else, the boys were fine. However, the moment someone else became the center of attention, our kids felt unloved and began vying for our attention.

Actually, it begins at birth. One can observe even in a newborn that a child measures the love of a parent in terms of the amount of attention the parent will provide.

Examining the quantity and quality of attention that someone pays to another person is an excellent gauge for measuring that person's love, and it holds true for both animate and inanimate objects. For example, my neighbor collects and restores vintage automobiles. Every night he can be found in his garage, polishing or tinkering with his newest acquisition. If he is not physically working on a vehicle, he is

reading books or magazines about cars. Judging from the amount of
attention that he gives to those cars, it is safe to say that my neighbor
loves his cars. It would also come as no surprise if his wife were to
admit to feeling that he loves his cars more than he loves her.

Attention, Not Time

Love is measured by the amount of attention, not by the amount of
time spent together. Commuting to work is one of those things that
many of us spend time doing. However, I do not love driving; it is only
a means to an end. While on the road, I daydream, fade in and out,
paying only enough attention to ensure my safety and that of other
drivers.

On the other hand, there are those activities, like wrestling with my
two boys. Doing this does not take up huge amounts of my time, yet
during those brief moments I am completely absorbed in our play.
Their giddy excitement and raucous laughter make me forget about
everything else. It does not take a rocket scientist (or a psychologist) to
figure out which activity I love and which one I only tolerate. The
difference is that I give my full attention to one, while I give as little as
possible to the other.

Someone may live in the garage, but that does not make him or her
a car. We can clock years, even decades, of time in our marriages, but
that does not mean we love each other. Love is based on how much
attention we bring. Simply being in the same room or the same house
with our spouse does not convey the feeling of love. It is being
attentive when we are together that truly measures affection.

Attention Is How We Communicate Love

Maybe it is one of those "guy" things, but I am notorious for
waiting until the last minute to get Lynda a birthday or anniversary
present. Depending on how "last minute" it is, I may have the store
clerk wrap it. Otherwise, I will stick it in one of those gift bags and
cover it with the same paper she used for one of my gifts last
Christmas. When I give it to her she appreciates it, but it does not

blow her away, no matter how much money I spend. By contrast, when Wesley produces a gold painted macaroni necklace that he made for her at school, Lynda is moved to tears.

For the longest time, I could not figure out what I was doing wrong. "Maybe I'm not getting her something she wants." When the next big event rolled around, I gave her the new dishwasher she had been eyeing. Again she was grateful, but she did not jump up and down.

I did not see that I was working from my own definition of love. I would have loved it if someone had given me a new power tool or had spent a lot of money on me. Therefore, I could not understand why she was not ecstatic over the dishwasher.

It did not occur to me until much later that I was not investing any of myself into the gift. By waiting until the last minute to pick up something, letting the salesperson wrap it, and by carelessly stuffing it into a bag, I was demonstrating my lack of attention. No matter that the gift itself was something she really wanted, my under-investment of energy, time and thoughtful consideration came across to Lynda as an indication that I was not giving of myself. I had not brought concentrated attention to the process of giving. Therefore, there was no love communicated through the gift.

In the early years of our relationship I had, indeed, found that if I went shopping a week before the occasion and perhaps wrapped the gift myself—even though it might not be a perfect wrapping job—my thoughtful gestures communicated to Lynda as much as my gifts that I loved her. She could feel and deeply appreciate my gifts of time and attention.

Exercise- See For Yourself

The attention we give our partner is even more important in communicating love than the words we use.
Try telling your partner how much you love him/her while you are reading a book or working on the computer.

Without looking at her/him, express how much you care in a flat voice.

Do it again the next day, but this time bring him/her as much attention as you can generate. Use the same words as you did before, but this time, be completely attentive.

Wait for a moment when you and your partner have some free time. If you have to create a circumstance to be together by going on a walk or planning a dinner out, that is fine. However, most importantly, make sure the TV is off, mute will not do. Now, shift your focus off yourself and focus completely on your spouse. Remember what it is you love about your mate. Take a minute or two to study his/her features. Make eye contact. Touch your spouse's arm and express your affection through physical connection. Neither of you may be accustomed to so much attention, so be playful with it, and give as much as feels comfortable. Then repeat the same loving comments as before.

As you allow yourself to play with this gift of attention, note your lover's response as well as your own. *You will find that not only does attention communicate love, it creates love.*

As you focus attention on your partner you will not only create an intimate moment for him/her, but also that gift of attention will open your heart. Attention communicates love to our partner and also stimulates our own loving feelings. *It is this gift of attention that enables us to truly "make love."*

Attention Is How We Create Love

Kirk never felt close to his in-laws. Even worse, they knew it. There was nothing wrong with Sally's parents, they were both very good people, but he did not have a lot in common with them. He was a "white collar" worker, while both of them were more "blue collar." Yet, that probably was not the core of it.

Early in their courtship, Sally and Kirk had talked about their childhood and the difficulties each had with their parents. As he listened to Sally's stories, he built up some resentment. To Sally, they were her parents, so when her folks were around she was able to "forgive and forget," leaving history in the past. Kirk, though, found it a lot more difficult to let go of his acquired resentment and to accept them—he did not have the bond that she had. Actually, when compared to his own parents, his in-laws were saints, and yet it was easier for Kirk to be angry with her parents than it was to be angry with his own.

After being in counseling with Sally, he began to realize that his ten years of smoldering resentment toward his in-laws was wrong. Kirk also recognized that nothing would ever change unless he changed. So, the next time Sally's parents came to visit, Kirk made it a point to practice love with them by giving them his complete attention. It did not matter if he did not relate to what they were saying. He simply gave them his undivided attention, really listening to them.

After the visit was over, Kirk noticed two things: not only did his in-laws appear more motivated to talk with him, but also he felt more interested in hearing what they had to say.

His heart had begun to open, and he slowly had realized that he felt more caring and compassionate towards them. Gradually, throughout the day, the uncomfortable resentments had disappeared and the interactions had begun to feel more relaxed— not only to Kirk but also to his visitors. By the end of the evening, he was experiencing a positive connection with both of them that had never existed before.

~

They had not changed. They were exactly who they had always been. It was his attitude that was different. This transformation was not a "magical answer" that had come without effort. It was more like charging a re-chargeable battery. When Kirk focused his attention on his in-laws, a "charge," a familiarity and a strong bond developed and he felt closer to them. But when he let his attention wander, even for just a few moments, he could sense the relationship reverting back (battery discharging) into a state of polite distance.

As a corollary to the battery analogy, once the initial connection with his in-laws was made, it did not require Kirk's constant attention to maintain it. He discovered that he could still spend time giving attention to his own needs without damaging or severing the relationship that was building up. However, he also realized that if he did not consciously return his attention, at least intermittently, to nurturing the relationship, the closeness would again begin to slip away.

To help you experience what Kirk did with his in-laws, let me give you an exercise to play with. The activity is called the *One Minute Miracle*. You will find it on the next page.

Exercise- The One Minute Miracle

Before you begin this exercise, take a base-line reading on your feelings of connection. Rate how close you feel to your intimate partner on a scale from zero to ten, *with ten meaning you are feeling completely in love, while a one on the scale would be like roommates, or a zero, strangers.*

Now choose a favorite picture of your spouse and find a place where you can be undisturbed for 5 minutes. Sit in a comfortable place and become aware of your breathing. Begin to notice how your exhaled breath naturally releases tension and relaxes the body. Use the next five or six exhaled breaths to let go of any negative feelings in your body or your mind. If there are points of tension that do not seem to release easily, exaggerate the tightness by constricting the muscles even tighter and holding it for five seconds. Then again, with an exhaled breath, release and relax the muscle. Tighten and loosen as many times as needed until you are feeling calm and at peace.

Look at the picture of your intimate partner. If any negative feelings arise, use your exhaled breaths to release them. With your head and heart clear start bringing your partner your full attention. Study the photograph. Notice his eyes, her face, and his body in detail. Use the inhalations to draw in pleasant feelings. As you look at your beloved for the next minute or two, continue the cycle of breathing in the good feelings and breathing out the bad. Imagine touching her, holding his hand, or kissing her. Whisper his name repeatedly with each breath, or think it with the tongue of the mind. It works best to say it quietly, but saying your mate's name to yourself is fine. After completing several breaths using his name, add the phrase "I love you", and continue to give her your full regard for another minute. Finish with a kiss to the picture, or simply imagine giving him a kiss.

When you have finished, rate again those feelings of closeness on a scale of 0 to 10. Notice any changes. If you did not feel a shift, go back and note how much attention was available for the activity. The more energy and attention you can bring to the exercise the more effective it will be. It is not uncommon for people to report to me that after doing this assignment they have an irresistible urge to call their spouse or walk over to where they are and give them a hug. If your mate is nearby, please do so.

As we initially walk through this activity it will take three to five minutes. When you get more familiar with the process this time will be shorten to one minute. The first fifteen seconds you will use your breath to calm and center yourself. The next fifteen seconds you will visualize or look at a picture of your partner. Imagine touching and holding your mate for the next fifteen seconds. Finally stimulate the auditory sections of your brain by spending the last quarter repeating his or her name and saying, "I love you."

This exercise is called *The One Minute Miracle* because by spending one minute at a time, three times a day, you will begin to feel a complete transformation of your marriage. Practice the exercise for the next week, and by the end of that time you will probably feel closer, conversations will happen more easily and spontaneously, and your sex life will again begin to catch fire.

Where Our Love Was Lost

When Lynda and I did not understand love, it was a complete mystery to us that relationships changed so dramatically and sometimes quickly—those of others, and ours, too. After a few years of marriage, couples can go from loving to loathing. Most of us married because we could not stand being apart. Ironically, people get divorced because they cannot stand being together. At the beginning, they loved every little thing about their partner, but something changed and now it is those same "little things" that irritate them. One day the love was there and the next day it was not.

Once we grasp the link between attraction and regard, it becomes obvious why and how feelings of connection change. Attention is drawn to novelty. The ebb and flow of any marriage corresponds with our focus and regard. Things that are new grab us and hold our attention effortlessly. Thus, a couple's feelings are never stronger than they are in the dating years. Once the two are married and the newness begins to wear thin, so may their affection for one another decline.

When Lynda and I were dating, everything between us was new and fresh, and as the relationship progressed, each stage brought a sense of ever-increasing excitement. We dated, became a couple, were engaged, and finally we married. Each stage brought a sense of renewal to the relationship. However, once we were married, everything that was new and different now lived outside the relationship. Our careers, our new home, and the needs of the children all started competing for our attention, so we spent less and less time tending to each other.

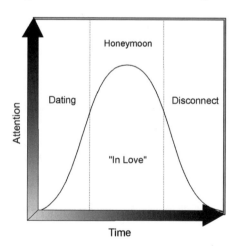

This waning of attention correlates perfectly with a decline in our feelings of affection. Our attention was diverted and, as a result, our feelings of love slowly dissipated. The commitment and desire to be together never changed, yet the day-to-day experience of love seemed to dry up. We take our mates for granted. We assume that love will last without nurturing. Like a plant, love needs to be watered for it to continue to thrive.

You can find the most exciting roller coaster and the first few times on the ride are completely exhilarating. Nevertheless, if you continue to ride it repeatedly, you find the ride does not hold your concentration. As the ride begins its clickity-clack up the hill, your mind begins wandering off, thinking about other rides. It does not matter how exciting it was in the beginning, everything becomes routine over time, including our relationships. Our loving feelings are lost if they are not continually renewed.

Exercise- Relationship Timeline

Truth is truth not because some authority said it was but because we can see it for ourselves. This next exercise will give the reader a chance to see the link between love and attention, as they chart the rise and fall of their feelings over the course of their relationship.

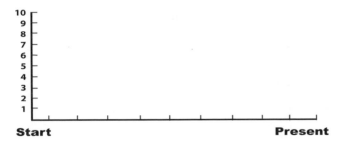

Take a piece of paper and lay it out horizontally. About an inch in from the margin draw a line from the top left hand corner down to the bottom left. Then run another line from the bottom left to the bottom right, again about an inch from the margin, as in the diagram above.
Place 10 evenly distributed marks on both the vertical and horizontal lines. Number the vertical lines from 1 to 10. This is going to be where you will rate your feelings

of connectedness with your partner. The number 1 means not connected, and 10 represents being completely in love. The longer horizontal line will be the time line. Divide this any way you like. The ten marks could represent the first ten years of marriage, or ten significant events, such as dating, engagement, marriage, first child, or a first home.

Begin rating your feelings of connection at the beginning of your relationship, or work backwards from today.
Shown below is how I rated my marriage with Lynda over our first ten years.

Lynda and I were closest on the day we got married. There was a dip in the first year; this was an adjustment period. After bouncing back in the second year, the marriage slowly declined until about our eighth year. With the discovery of love as attention, our feeling of closeness again rebounded and has continued to climb ever since.

When you complete the closeness rating, go back and use the same scale of 1 to 10, but this time rate the amount of attention you brought to each other over those years. One equates to "little to none," while 10 reflects that you were thinking of your spouse all the time. You may find, as I did, that the correlation between the feelings of connection and the amount of attention parallels perfectly.

We mistakenly believe that our commitment to the relationship is the same thing as a commitment to love. Showing up every day is just not enough to keep a marriage alive. A bond is created in the beginning of our relationship, but that bond will not carry on forever without being continually renewed. The only way to do that is with love.

Here is a poetic analogy that illustrates the point.

The tree of love is planted as a seedling in the heart of each of two people when they begin to bond in romantic relationship. As the relationship grows, so does that seedling. It is the ever-deepening roots of love's timber, drawing in the wonderful feelings and recording the shared experiences of life, that nourish, and strengthen the bond. When the awareness of that nourishing is present in their hearts, the light it generates permits lovers to see and feel the tree of love standing strong. At other times, though, their hearts may grow dark and their awareness may falter, but still they may know and trust that there is something substantial holding them together. So they take on faith the notion that they still love each other, even though they may not feel it in that moment.

One day, it may happen that the lovers return to their hearts, look inside, and discover that, for lack of attention to the difficult truth that constant nourishment is required, the tree of love has died. And they ask why.

You Can Be Right Or You Can Be Married®

The answer is that darkness of heart is created in the shadows of hurt or anger, moods and feelings that detract from loving attention and distract lovers from their need to nourish one another and the relationship. Thus, the tree of love withers and dies.

Attention is the substance that feeds all relationships and nourishes every soul. Love between humans is not a static state that, once established, lasts for eternity. Love requires daily sustenance, constant nourishment. Love is a living force that is not simply a commitment made sometime in the past. It is here, it is present, it is now, and it is worthy of attention in every moment, with every thought and action. Love is something we each need to foster with the gift of attention—or else it will leave us.

Homework: At least once every day for the next week take out your journal and rate how close you feel to your partner at that moment, on a scale from 1 to 10.
Then do The One Minute Miracle.
After completing the exercise, rate your feeling of connection again.
Note how it changes daily and weekly.

Chapter 7

The Free Gift of Attention

Discovering what it means
to have free attention

~

"Damn it, Helen! Why can't you just get off my back?"

~

Frank's angry outburst carries with it lots of attention and high intensity, but by no means does Helen feel loved.

During a workshop, someone will inevitably point out that although rage focuses us on our partner, it is not felt as affection. In the most general terms, love and attention are intricately locked, but there is a small qualifier that refines our definition. For our *regard* to be experienced as *fondness*, our consideration must be given freely. Love is, specifically, the *free gift* of our attention.

"To understand love as the free gift of our attention let us first examine the problem of self-focused misapplications of attention. The three distortions of our regard are: Perturbed, People Pleasing, and Puppy Love.

Perturbed

It is true that anger carries with it a large amount of energy and attention. Even if a person is not screaming, but rather is in a quiet sulk or pout, his or her thoughts are almost certainly focused on what happened that produced the hurt or upset out of which the anger grew. Even though the angry person's thoughts are directed toward the person who inflicted the injustice, no one would confuse that with love—neither the person feeling it nor the person receiving it.

The pertinent question is, "Where is the attention focused?" To what or to whom are we really giving our attention? When we are angry, our attention is, in fact, centered on ourselves. It is about how we feel hurt, betrayed, or neglected. Yes, an aggressive response may be directed at our mate, but our attention is really focused on ourselves and on a perceived violation.

Anger is ultimately rooted in our own thoughts and feelings. Thus, it is never confused by the other person as love. Quite the opposite, people who are excessively angry at the world are seen as self-absorbed, self-focused, and self-righteous.

Anger focuses our attention on ourselves.

When someone is annoyed, his or her attention is focused on the issue and not on the partner. The "love" being expressed is actually for him/herself, inasmuch as that is where his/her energy is fixated. There is nothing wrong with being angry. Feeling irritated or annoyed is a normal response to our purported hurts. The problem is that our anger tends to turn our attention back upon ourselves, which means withdrawing it from the other person. When couples become angry they withdraw attention from each other instead of giving attention to the other.

If giving our regard feels like love, then the absence of attention is felt as unlove. That is exactly what couples experience when they become angry with one another. Irritation directs our awareness on ourselves, and couples then stop attending to each other. This collapse of attention is experienced by each partner as a withdrawal of love by the other.

We do not give attention when we are angry. We tend to withhold it. Giving attention means being able to focus on someone else, to hear his/her frustration, to see the other person's point of view, and to feel our partner's pain. When we become angry with our partner, our focus is on our issues, not his/hers. This is why anger does not feel loving. Instead, it is experienced as abandonment or rejection.

Positive vs. Negative Attention

I remember being about four years old and watching my mother take my father's ukulele out of the car. She threw it on the ground and began stomping on it. My father stood by quietly and watched, never raising his voice. He did not say anything. The longer he did not react, the stronger my mother's reaction became.

Looking back on the situation, I can now see that my mother was starving for a connection with my father. I can only assume that all day she had been trying to get his attention and had failed. The "good" intent behind her bad behavior was to get him to yell at her. That is, to give her some kind of attention.

The strange thing about anger is that its negative energy or attention does simulate love, in that it does connect. However, the connection is negative. If we give enough attention we begin to "love to hate" whomever our anger is turned against.

People in general tend to think of attention as being positive or negative. Both kinds of attention will create a bond. The difference, of course, is that "positive" attention creates a loving/healthy bond, while "negative" attention brings two people together in unpleasant/unhealthy ways. I am sure that my mother intentionally provoked my father into a fight because it must have seemed better to her than the silence she was living with.

Even children will act out for attention because *negative attention is better than no attention at all.*

You see, *the opposite of love is not anger, it is apathy.* As we have stated before, it is not negative attention that translates into the experience of being unloved, it is the absence of any attention.

The fact that attention of any kind creates a bond can lead to the mis-perception that abuse is love or that rage and violence mean that someone cares. When people grow up in or enter a relationship absent of "positive" (or free) selfless attention, "negative" (or self-focused) attention may be interpreted as love.

Positive attention connects positively;

negative attention connects negatively.

People living in healthy relationships do not understand how someone could be abused and not only fail to press charges but also take back the perpetrator. The answer, it turns out, is another question: How can a woman have her husband arrested for loving her in the only way he or she understands?

Since the absence of attention is felt as a message of unlove, the woman wrongly believes, that if her partner were to stop hitting or yelling, she would enter a world of silence, isolation—and unlove. The need to love and be loved is stronger, at times, than even our need for safety. Hence, anger and conflict may be preferable to no attention at all.

It is undeniable that attention, in any form, bonds us with whomever we focus it upon. However, if we want that connection to be positive and loving, our attention needs to be free—free in every sense of the word. Our focus has to be given without any strings attached, free from negative energies such as anger. The experience of love comes through the gift of our free attention.

People Pleasers

When I was growing up I lived with only my father and my two brothers. There was a lot of masculine energy around the house. The "domestic" role was a niche that was left open. Over time, I began to fill this role. From an early age, I took it upon myself to play my father's "little helper." I would make meals, do the dishes, clean the living room, and try getting my brothers to toe the line. All of it was done in the hope of winning my father's approval. As time went on, I adopted this psuedo-caretaker role with everyone—peers, teachers, and even other caretakers like my mother and grandmother. As a result, I became an expert people pleaser, all the time praying that if I took care of everyone else someone would then take care of me.

I found it very confusing when no one seemed to reciprocate but instead became irritated. My father did not go out of his way to meet my needs. Rather than feeling grateful that I was picking up the slack, Dad was annoyed with my attempts to "help" run the family.

For attention to be felt as love

it must be given freely.

Even as a very young boy I understood that there was a relationship between attention and love. However, I did not know that for attention to be experienced as love, it had to be given as a free gift, without a hidden agenda. The motive behind my giving affection by "helping" was to win the affection of those around me. Because I did not give my gift freely, but used as a means to an end, my efforts were not perceived as loving, they were seen as manipulative.

Used car salesmen can be very attentive to the subtle cues and needs of a patron. "Can I get you some coffee?" "Those are some really cute kids." When this happens to you, do you perceive it as true affection? Probably not. You see them as attempts to win your business. Because my attentiveness had an ulterior motive, it was not experienced as caring but as annoying.

Puppy Love

The distinction between *self-focused* and *other-focused* attention explains the difference between infatuations (or crushes) and true love.

During our teenage years, it is common for us human beings to fall deeply and madly "in love." Whenever we are around the object of our affection the heart races, the mind gets a little fuzzy, and the knees grow weak. Remember? Those feelings of "love" seemed quite real, did they not?

But often, sometimes within only a few weeks, we would lose all interest. After a few dates, and maybe a few heartbreaks, we were done. The intense feelings of affection would vanish and we would tell our friends, "I am so over them." Where did the love go? How did it change so quickly? Normally, we think of love as something that is more stable than these whimsical flights into infatuation.

So . . . what was all that, if it was not love? We enjoy the fluttery feelings of excitement when a special person comes around. But these surges of hormones are nothing more than a fondness. Our attention is not focused on the other person. It is focused on how good we feel. In those moments of infatuation, we are in love with the feelings we are experiencing, not with the other person. We are in love with being "in love."

Do we love the other person

or is it how he or she makes us feel?

Attention must be free—no hidden agendas—free of negative feelings like anger, free even of our need to be loved in return. No strings, nothing focused back on ourselves. The more attention we can free up for our partner, the stronger will become our sense of love. If only a small amount of attention can be freed, then the bond will be minimal. The power and control rests within all of us. The choice is ours: *to love or not to love.*

Testing Whether Your Attention Is Free

The best way to find out if there is a hidden agenda behind your acts of concern is to examine those times when the outcome is not what you expected.

You Can Be Right Or You Can Be Married®

In one scene from the movie "The Fisher King," Jeff Bridges gives Robin Williams a $100 bill. The Bridges character is trying to clear his conscience by offering Williams (who is playing a street person) some cash. The Williams character takes the money, but he immediately gives it to another homeless man. Bridges, the baffled donor, begins a fight to get his money back. The point, of course, is that if the money had been a real gift it would not matter what the other person might choose to do with it.

Notice your own response when you do a kind act and the recipient does not respond or does not seem pleased. If the recipient's response stirs a fire within you, then you were almost certainly expecting something very specific in return—a kind word, praise, or some acknowledgment. Your upset and discomfort reveal that you did, indeed, have an agenda—the gift was not freely given, after all.

Small children continually demand the free gift of unconditional love and attention from their parents. They want mom and dad to be responsive to their every need and desire. However, the children have not yet learned about grateful response or other socially acceptable gestures. They know that their parents will keep on caring for them even when they call their parents names, hit, bite or spit. We discipline our children, teaching them about behaviors that are appropriate or not appropriate, but we do not withdraw our attention, our caring, or our love. We do not tell them, "I'm done; I'm not going to care for you any more."

As with the process of raising small children, at times in our grown-up relationships we need to discipline and to set limits and boundaries with our intimate partners, but in order to be successful in doing so we must do it in a spirit of love. We cannot offer our affection as a reward for doing what we ask, nor can we withhold it if our partner does not comply.

This, then, is the defining characteristic of a successful relationship: that each person continually brings attention to his/her partner. Even in a good marriage we may get hurt or frustrated with one another, there may be misunderstandings and moments of anger. But when the difficulties arise, we do not withdraw our regard. In healthy relationships, troublesome emotions like anger, hurt, or disappointment do not collapse our energy and cause us to flee, either emotionally or physically. We may let our partner know about our upset, but the emotions do not dam up or restrict our flow of attention.

Redefining a Successful Marriage

Scientific research supports the idea that the giving of free attention, or love, makes a relationship successful. John Gottman, Ph.D., a research scientist from Washington State University, has analyzed couples in controlled laboratory situations for the past 20 years. His findings have been published in numerous journal articles and books, including *The Marriage Clinic—A Scientifically-Based Marital Therapy,* the collective volume of his years of research[viii]. From that work, Gottman has arrived several radical and surprising conclusions.

First, he finds that good communication does not represent the hallmark of a healthy marriage. He demonstrates instead that the characteristic distinguishing a flourishing relationship from one that is failing is, of all things, attention. Conventional wisdom, as expressed through the science/art of psychology, tells us that good communication builds good relationships. Gottman's studies of married couples do not bear this out. His research has revealed that some 70% of all conflicts are "unresolvable." Evidence of this includes the finding that the vast majority of the arguments between marital partners are repetitive—the disagreements they had a year ago are the same general issues they are arguing about today and will be fighting over a year from now.

70% of all conflicts are unresolvable.

Disagreements over family finances, differences relating to childrearing, and household responsibilities are topics that continually plague a marriage because they are subjects that are "unresolvable."

Year after year, the same arguments occur. There seem to be no answers or solutions. According to Gottman, the best a couple may be able to do in this circumstance, is first to be heard, then to agree to disagree.

~

Phil, a close friend of mine, was planning to celebrate his 20th anniversary with his wife by renewing their marriage vows. In preparation, Phil began reading through some of the journals he had written two decades earlier, when he and his wife were dating. All at once, he was surprised to read about an argument they had shortly before their wedding—an argument they had repeated the previous evening! Phil, by the way, is a licensed psychologist who makes communication his life. Clearly, the issue that was the central focus of their two arguments—almost 20 years apart—is not something that simply needs to be discussed. It is a part of their personalities that was not going to disappear.

~

Gottman focuses on creating a "positive set" with couples. He defines a healthy marriage one which achieves a favorable response rate to one another's "bid" for attention. Throughout the day, two people will continually seek each other's regard. Successful relationships are measured by how the two respond to one another's bids.

There are three possible responses, according to Dr. Gottman's findings. The responder can

1)   turn toward a bid,

2)   turn away from it, or

3)   turn against it.

~

Susan comments, "Isn't it a beautiful morning?" Her remark is seen as a bid for Larry's, attention. Larry can choose from one of the three basic responses.

- He may turn toward her bid for attention by replying, "Yes it is gorgeous."

- He may turn away by not replying at all.

- Or he may go on the attack. "It would be a lot nicer if you were not always talking."

The enthusiastic reply is defined as "turning toward," while the lack of a response is a turning away. A turning against is, of course, seen in the last comment.

~

Gottman has found that healthy couples have a generally supportive response to each other's bids for attention. On average, 91% of the time, well-adjusted couples will respond enthusiastically. By contrast, unhealthy couples turn away or turn against their partners nearly 80% of the time.

Couples that bring positive attention to each other thrive. It does not matter whether or not all of the issues between them are resolved. The determinant is that a couple be warm and affectionate with each other in most of their interactions.

Dr. Gottman believes, as I do, that happy marriages are characterized by the amount of attention couples bring to one another. Communication is overrated. It is the consistent gift of our regard that maintains our bonds.

Homework: Practice being conscious of your partner. Find some way to serve your spouse that he or she will not know about. If shopping is not a normal activity you do for the household, then pick up an item at the market. Do something out of the ordinary, like organize a bookshelf, but do it without being noticed. Any action that is out of your normal routine will help be mindful of your partner. Because it is unsolicited, it will prevent you from having expectations, thus making the attention free.

Chapter 8

The Three Types of Attention

Finding the kind of attention
our partner wants

Rejected

~

Steve complains that every time he tries to love his wife, Julie, she pushes him away. "I hold her hand or get close to her on the couch, and she will tolerate me for a few moments, but then she gets irritated and pulls away." When I ask Steve about what kind of attention his wife wants, he comments, "All Julie seems to care about is keeping the house clean. If I vacuum the living room she's happy, but that does nothing for building our relationship."

~

We have already recognized that if strings are attached to our attention it is experienced more like manipulation than love. What needs to be developed further is the process of gifting. A true gift must be something our partner can recognize and appreciate. Steve's difficulty with Julie boils down to the issue that *the attention he is giving is not something she wants*. Steve enjoys holding, touching and caressing. Julie, on the other hand, wants some help around the house.

Instead of bringing attention in a form Julie needs, Steve brings her the kind of attention he wants.

Not all attention is the same. The simple directive to bring attention to one another is not clear enough. It is like saying, "Go to the corner and turn." Which way? To say that attention needs to be positive is not specific enough. "Positive for whom?" If it is only positive attention, then how can we be constructive or set limits and continue to love? To simply say love is positive attention is like saying, "Go to the corner and turn safely." The directive to be positive is appropriate enough, but it does not clarify in what direction to head.

Instead, if we say, "Go to the corner and turn away from the tall elm, and toward the yellow house," it does not matter if you are going north or south, the instruction works well in both directions. Likewise, for love to be felt and received, our attention must be focused away from ourselves and toward the other person. There is no right or left, right or wrong; the more we turn our attention away from ourselves and give it to our partner, the more love our partner experiences.

Comparing Apples and Oranges

The problem is that couples are comparing apples to oranges. I really enjoy a good apple. I love the rich color, the loud crunch, and the sweet flavor of a fresh apple. As a gesture of love I offer my partner a piece of my favorite fruit, and when she is not interested or pushes my gift away I feel hurt/unloved.

It is not that my partner does not love me. My partner likes oranges. She enjoys their juice and wonderful smell. In fact, she feels hurt that I did not give her an orange. In turn, when she offers me an orange, my disinterest is felt as a lack of caring—not for the orange but for her. To reject her gift is to reject her.

The attention we bring must match the kind of attention our partner needs.

It is clear that the gifting of attention, the receiving and returning of love, makes a relationship happy and healthy. It is not as clear that different people bring attention to the relationship in different ways. Simply bringing attention is not good enough. The attention has to be something the other person needs and wants. It may be cute for one of my boys to give his mother a Matchbox car. However, if *I* give my wife a new DVD system or a power tool of some kind, she will not see it as cute.

Couples are continually giving and getting attention from one another, but too often that thoughtfulness is not perceived by the person toward whom the attention is directed because it comes in a form that is indecipherable. A classic example is the man who works long hours and, consequently, is away from the house for many hours each working day. He sees himself as "doing it for the family." His wife, on the other hand, may compare the amount of time he gives his job verses the energy he devotes to their home and conclude that he loves his job more than he loves the family.

One person in the relationship may value a peaceful home and thus will work at bringing calm and quiet, while to the other person in the marriage may perceive this conflict avoidance as an expression of distancing and "not caring." Men often view their home handyman skills as a gift to their family, whereas women often interpret it as something the man does so as to avoid interacting with the family.

The same misunderstanding of the intention behind attention sometimes happens when a woman gives attention to her spouse and the family by cleaning, while her spouse would much rather have cuddle time. The emphasis on housekeeping may be perceived as compulsive, self-gratifying, or even as the same kind of avoidance mechanism as the "handyman syndrome".

The inability to bring attention in a way the other person values is experienced as unlove. If I know what makes my wife happy, which flowers she enjoys versus the flowers that she is allergic to, then she feels that I love her. Therefore, part of the gift must be that we pay enough attention to know the difference.

Visual, Auditory, and Kinesthetic

Each human being is hard-wired to access and process information in one or more of three primary sensory styles. People process information either through sight, sound, or touch. Nowhere has this been studied more than in the educational field. Teachers at all grade levels have known for years that children take in information—or attend to different stimuli—through these three basic modalities: visual, auditory, and kinesthetic.

To help children learn, teachers and curriculum developers adapt their materials to include all three of these modalities because research has shown that even though we have and use all of these senses to gather information, each of us tends to have a dominant modality. One student may rely on my visual sense and require handouts, while another pupil may be primarily an auditory learner and will therefore rely on verbal instruction.

Visual learners will comprehend most fully if they can see the material, auditory learners need to be told what to do, and kinesthetic learners need hands-on experiences or demonstrations to aid their learning process. A teacher who understands how each child in a classroom processes information can, therefore, communicate new ideas in such a way that a given child can grasp it more quickly and completely.

Adults are no different. Everyone has a mode in which he or she attends best. The style in which I best receive attention may not be the way my partner looks for it. The problem is not only that we fail to bring attention but also that the attention we bring is not valued—or perhaps not even noticed—by our partner. Often, auditory people miss the visual clues their partners use. Likewise, the kinesthetic person may be attentive in physical ways, but his or her visual partner fails to see any of these actions as signs of affection.

Testing Your Style

Here is a brief exercise that may help you clarify how you take in information.

Recall your very best day. It could have been your wedding, during a family vacation, your first child's birthday, when you moved into your first home, or a time spent in nature. Think about the day in as much detail as possible, remembering as much as you can. Picture the details of the scene, the objects in the room, the color of the floor, or the foliage and bright blue sky if you were outside. Notice how you were dressed. Think about the pleasant sounds that filled your ears: laughter, the soft voice of someone you love, music, the sound of water, or a breeze rustling the leaves. Were you standing, sitting, walking or lying down? Remind yourself of the feelings you had: relaxed, happy, loving, joyful, or peaceful.

In the margin of this page, write down what details were the strongest. Was it easier to remember the kind and loving words that were spoken? Or were the rich colors and details of the scene the easiest to recall? Could you feel the feeling within your own body again?

If you can easily picture the detail of the day, your primary sensory modality is probably visual. If the words that were spoken or sounds that you heard become your dominant memory, then you are an auditory person. A kinesthetic individual will remember how things felt, both physically and emotionally.

Even the selection of what was remembered will be different for these three types of processors.

The visual person will pick a pleasant memory based on the beauty of the day or the environment, such as a sunset in Hawaii.

By contrast, an auditory person will recall what was said and, in fact, may pick an image because of the loving messages that was expressed that day.

For the kinesthetic person, the beauty around them or what was said would not have been as important as the feelings that were felt. The memory he/she selected would have been based on the strong emotions experienced in his/her scene.

For some who tried this exercise, two or even all three modes may have been easy to use. Do not pigeonhole yourself into believing there is only one way of taking in information. There may be one area that is stronger than another, or there may be several strong areas.

The intent of the experience is to make the reader attune to where the attention is focused. Understanding where your attention is focused will give insight into the most effective ways you will feel loved.

To better understand how your partner processes information, simply look at how your spouse learns. Strike up a conversation about high school experiences. What does your partner remember best? Was it the lectures, the books that were read, the activities of a school day? For some it will be remembered as getting their hands dirty or the memory of visual aids, while for others, listening was what worked best.

Understand what your partner needs by learning how he or she learns.

Most people learn in all three modes but tend to favor one over the other two. That dominant modality becomes the "style" of each person's learning and understanding, the primary way in which new ideas are processed. In fact, learning occurs best when the information can be processed in more than one modality. To see it, hear it, and try it not only covers all the bases but reinforces the information.

To further clarify exactly the modality in which each person in the relationship operates, take a moment to complete the *Attention-Reception Test* on the following pages.

Love-Based Solutions For Couples^{SM}

Attention-Reception Test

Rate each item from 0 to 5 (0=strongly disagree, 5=strongly agree) for yourself and then for your spouse. Total each section. The highest total of the three sections will indicate the primary modality for each of you, while the second highest score will be the back-up modality. The lowest score will be the weakest modality.

First, the visual modality

Self	Spouse/Partner	
_____	_____	Gets irritated at clutter
_____	_____	Uses words such as "look", "see"
_____	_____	Learns best by seeing it done/handouts
_____	_____	Dresses well
_____	_____	Neat handwriting
_____	_____	Creates lists
_____	_____	Neat, meticulous, likes order
_____	_____	Impatient when extensive listening is required
_____	_____	Remembers faces, forgets names
_____	_____	Uses landmarks to explain directions
_____	_____	Pictures things clearly in his/her head
_____	_____	Good at puzzles, reading maps
_____	_____	Eyes move upward and to one side when thinking
_____	_____	Quiet when angry

Visual total score: Self: _____ Spouse: _____

Next, the auditory modality

Self	Spouse/Partner	
_____	_____	Distracted by sounds
_____	_____	Uses words such as "listen", "hear"
_____	_____	Good at following oral instructions
_____	_____	Enjoys music/quiet
_____	_____	Talks
_____	_____	Uses TV or radio for background noise
_____	_____	Repeats directions
_____	_____	Talks to self

_____	_____	Remembers names, forgets faces
_____	_____	Hums
_____	_____	Recalling what was said by whom
_____	_____	Learns by listening, radio, lectures, tapes
_____	_____	Moves eyes to the side when thinking
_____	_____	Verbal when angry

Auditory total score: Self: _____ Spouse: _____

Finally, the kinesthetic modality

Self   Spouse/Partner

_____	_____	Agitated if not active while listening
_____	_____	Uses words like "feel" , "get" and "take"
_____	_____	Learns by doing
_____	_____	Talks with his/her hands
_____	_____	Likes comfort over beauty
_____	_____	Shuts down when not stimulated
_____	_____	Touches things
_____	_____	Good with his/her hands
_____	_____	Likes hugs and physical closeness
_____	_____	Fidgets and moves a lot
_____	_____	Appears disorganized
_____	_____	Not bothered by messes
_____	_____	Moves eyes down when thinking
_____	_____	Active when angry

Kinesthetic total score: Self: _____ Spouse: _____

Summary Scores

PRIMARY MODALITY PREFERENCE

    Self: _____   Spouse: _____

BACK-UP MODALITY PREFERENCE

    Self: _____   Spouse: _____

Note how similar or dissimilar your individual totals are. When your three totals are, say, 38 (visual), 8 (auditory), and 51 (kinesthetic), it means that you are a strongly physical person, with the visual modality as a moderate back up. The low auditory scale indicates that verbal instruction is lost. If two of the scores are close, for example the auditory and visual totals being 48 & 47, then either modality could be used to re-connect.

This information is important to a relationship because the mode of learning that is dominant for each of you will let you know how you and your partner will best process or recognize each other's attention. A kinesthetic person may not readily process information that is relayed verbally. Because of this, he/she will not hear praise. Statements of "I love you" do not mean as much as touching or holding hands. The kinesthetic partner is not as likely to express feelings verbally but would rather demonstrate affection through cleaning, working, or getting physical.

Sue enters the living room modeling a dress for an evening out. "So, what do you think?"

Bill comments, "It's nice," as he momentarily glances up from the computer.

"I'm not sure I like it," Sue responds. After a moment or two she continues, "Would my black dress look better?"

"That would be fine too," he answers back. His blank stare makes it painfully clear to Sue that the computer is winning the battle for Bill's attention.

Sue questions him again. "What about wearing the red one?"

After a two second delay, he responds again, "That would be all right."

At that point Sue explodes in anger, "I don't have a red dress! If you love that computer so much, why don't you take it out to dinner? I'm not going!"

The sad part of this story is that Bill's intentions were good, but his choice of how to express them fell short. He understood that he needed to bring Sue his attention, and, in fact, he was on the computer creating a CD of all their favorite songs for their date. Since he was an auditory person, he could remember all their favorite music and was choosing to express his attention in this way. However, he had no visual memory for what color dresses Sue had in her wardrobe. So, he paid little attention to what she was asking him, not realizing that her questions were simply designed to meet her own needs.

Each of them was bringing a particular kind of energy to the evening. Sue wanted to look attractive for Bill, to please him with her appearance. Her hope was to let him know she loved him by looking nice for their evening together. Bill, too, wanted to express his affection, but it was through music. The point is that each of them was bringing attention, but it was missed because the attention was not tuned to a frequency where the other person could see it (or hear it, or feel it, depending on his or her point of view).

This situation between Yolanda and Oscar further illustrates the point.

~

Yolanda would continually tell Oscar, "I would be happy if you could just give me a dandelion and a post-it note." She was forever after Oscar to get her flowers or give her a card as a sign that she was loved. Oscar spent most of his weekends repairing and improving things around the house, such as lights and leaky faucets. Yolanda, too, spent time straightening, doing the laundry, and cleaning up dishes, but she did not put much thought into it because it was simply something that had to be done.

Oscar was incensed at being accused of not caring simply because he never brought flowers. He saw what he did at work during the week and taking care of things around the house on the weekends as his way of bringing attention to the family. One mode is not a more legitimate means of love than another, but the fight between Oscar and Yolanda stemmed from the fact that they had their attention placed on different forms of attention/love.

⌒

The giving of attention begins with learning what is meaningful to our partner. The gift has to be something our partner wants. Change for Sue and Bill, or for Oscar and Yolanda, would be as simple as learning to tune into the frequency on which the other person operates.

Bringing some attention to how Sue looked would have gone a long way for Bill. In the same way, if Sue had been aware of Bill's need for soft loving tones and praise, she would have been able to easily communicate her love for him in such a way that he could hear.

Yolanda could not see if the plumbing under the sink was leaking or not, so she did not see any visual signs of Oscar's love. Fixing things around the house was a great way for Oscar to demonstrate his devotion, but it meant more to him than it did to Yolanda. If he had wanted to leave Yolanda feeling cared for, then he would have needed to create a visible symbol.

Our attention has to be

a gift that our partner wants.

Paying attention to what our partner needs and wants is the first gift or step in strengthening our bond. The second stage is to then learn how to bring attention in his/her style.

Homework: Spend the next few days bringing attention to your partner in a variety of different means. Notice which style of attention your partner receives best.

Section Three

REINFORCE
The Practice of Love[SM]

Part One of The Practice of Love
Loving Our Intimate Partner

Throughout history, religious and spiritual traditions have urged that we should love our neighbor as we love ourselves.

This section will teach couples about how to love their partners, and in turn create a greater sense of relatedness.

Chapter 9

Giving, Caring, and Talking

Feeding your relationship

The Perfect Gift

It was two weeks before Christmas, and I thought I would practice love by not doing my typical last minute dash through the mall. I was looking for a unique gift for Lynda that would convey to her how special she was to me. After several days of searching, having come up with nothing, I mentally "clicked on" when Lynda commented that she needed a new calendar. It was the idea I was looking for.

On the following Saturday, the boys and I went through a tub of duplicate pictures Lynda had in storage. The boys found a few dozen photos of themselves and the family, and we grouped them into themes. We tried to cluster the photos in such a way that they would correspond with the different holidays and seasons throughout the year. Then we snuck into Lynda's scrap booking materials and collected stickers and backgrounds that complimented our twelve themes. Working an hour or so every day, the project took almost a week to put together. Once it was done the groups of photos were taken to a printer who produced a calendar, just in time for Christmas.

Lynda loved it! The calendar was her favorite gift. And the most revealing thing I learned from that experience was that by the end of the project I also felt loving and connected. Spending all that time woke me up to how detached I had been over the last few months, and it helped me re-attach my heart to hers.

What to Do with Feeling Unloved

Thus far we have identified that the trouble with our relationships stems from a mood of unlove. The obvious solution would be to get our partner to give us the kind of attention we crave. When we feel unloved, our first thought is about how to direct our partner into taking care of our needs. A more effective means for feeling loved is to love.

The typical solution is to focus outside of ourselves as a way to address our unhappiness within. The material world tells us that we can fulfill our emptiness by getting more stuff—a new car, a house, a big TV set—when we feel any kind of lack in our life. To feel loved, we believe we need to be loved. The answer to our unhappiness, we think, is to go out and get happiness from the people and things around us.

The fantasy that "being loved"

will cure our lovelessness

fosters our feelings of betrayal.

This solution, to be loved, as a cure for our mood of unlove, sets us up once again for our Right Fights. Anything that is said with a view to changing our partner—or trying to get him or her to do something—is not communicating, it is correcting. If we focus on our spouse's behaviors, then our spouse will have to admit he or she fell short before we will get what we want. When our attention carries with it the hidden agenda of getting our spouse's attention, *our spouse does not see our behaviors as love but as manipulation.*

Let's go back and look at the problem again to see if we can find a better answer. The problem, we have discovered, is not that our partner does not love us but that *we* do not love. Our tendency to focus on what our partner is doing wrong keeps us stuck in our Right Fights. Yes, our spouse has done or not done, said or not said, something that has hurt our feelings. But to focus on how he or she has failed does not work. We need to focus on what *we* are doing or feeling.

In reviewing the problem, there is an intermediate step that we have not yet addressed—our own recoil. When we feel wounded or wronged, we tend to withdraw. We are not accountable for our partner's behavior, but we are culpable for our own actions. Our retreat from the other person kills the opportunity for communication from our side. Consequently, it is something that we are responsible for. We need to alter our "natural" impulse to retreat by doing the opposite and moving close. Loving—or bringing attention—must be the first step in restoring the relationship.

Connecting and protecting are mutually exclusive. Thus, by giving our regard and expressing our love, we overcome the more "natural" impulse to pull away.

The initial stage in practicing love is not to ask to be loved. it is to love. The logic appears counter-intuitive. By analogy, if my car is low on gasoline, giving away what little gas I have does not make any sense. In our relationship, a focus on connection is difficult when there is conflict because we feel, in that moment, unloved. How is *giving* love going to change our feelings of lovelessness?

Fortunately, love is more like a flower than a petroleum product. There are many flowers that deliver more and more fragrant blooms each time they are cut back. So it is with giving love. As we noted in the previous section, to give attention also creates and enhances the feeling of love within ourselves. Love is very different from any other human emotion. Love has the strange—yet deliciously wonderful—quality of feeling the same whether we are giving it or receiving it.

My kids enjoy hiding behind doors or furniture, lying in wait for an unsuspecting passerby and then jumping out, hoping to scare their mother or me—or a guest in our home. The satisfaction the boys get from seeing the look of surprise on their victim's face is very different from the feeling of being frightened; in other words, being scared is not the same experience as scaring someone. Similarly, being angry is not at all the same as experiencing someone else's anger when it is directed at you.

Love, however, feels the same whether I am behaving in a loving way toward my partner or my intimate partner is behaving lovingly toward me.

Love feels the same whether you are giving or receiving it.

In preparing Lynda's Christmas present—her calendar—I experienced loving warmth and excitement long before she ever knew about the gift.

Undoubtedly, the quickest cure for feelings of unlove is to love. At the root of all our conflicts is a feeling of hurt that translates into a mood of "you don't love me." The standard protocol for handling such emotions is to convince our partner he or she has done something wrong and thus to get him or her to never hurt us again. We all know how well that works!

The alternative course of action—the one that works—is to love, because love feels the same when we are giving it as when we are receiving it. Before dealing with our failure to communicate, the feelings of unlove that make communication impossible must be undone through the free gift of our attention.

The Three Staples

Life does not exist without continual renewal. We would die if we were to stop breathing for as little as five minutes. Failing to drink fluids for more than three days would threaten our existence. If we were to fast for less than a month, our bodies would fail. Every living

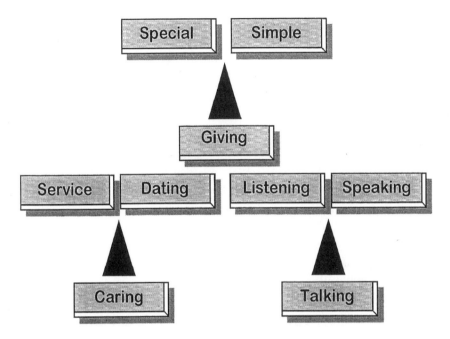

thing requires continual replenishment. To keep love alive it, too, must be constantly nourished. As breathing, drinking, and eating revitalize our flesh, so does giving, caring, and talking revitalize marriage.

The Relationship Timeline exercise in Chapter 6 verifies that our feelings of affection flourish or fade based on how much we nurture the relationship. It also demonstrates there is a dramatic difference in the amount and quality of attention that couples bring to one another when they are dating as compared to when they are married.

Dating couples tend to foster their feelings for each other in a variety of ways. There is more general giving, caring, and talking. When we get married however, not only does the volume of attention drop, but also the variety of ways in which we show our affection also kind of economy of energy. The result of our declining attention correlates perfectly with a decreased sense of connectedness.

To learn what our relationships hunger for, think back to those days when your love was more alive. Couples that feel a strong bond tend to express their affections tangibly, with presents, through their actions and activities, and in discussions. Giving, caring, and talking are the three staples that sustain the love and the life of any relationship.

Giving

Believe it or not, there are people out there who think that because they told their spouse they loved them on their wedding night, that expression should last them the rest of the relationship. "If it changes I will let you know. Otherwise, you can just always assume my feelings are there." The problem with this kind of thinking is that our feelings of affection are not static.

Love is an action.

Love is not only a noun. It is also a verb. Love is an action, an activity that needs to be continually expressed. The most noticeable way in which couples convey their affection for each other is in the gifts they give to one another. Presents are a tangible ways our partner can see and know that we care. When we think of these kinds of gifts we tend to think of something elaborate. Those big gifts are fine, of course, but our gift giving can also be small offerings that serve as frequent reminders of our love.

When discussing providing gifts of love to our partner, let us separate them into two categories: special and simple gifts. Special gifts are things we get for our partner that are out of the ordinary and are given on an occasional basis. Small presents, or even finding ways to give some attention to our partner, are simple gifts and should be given regularly.

Special Gifts

Men do well with special giving. When Christmas or Hanukkah rolls around, guys generally like to be heroic and make "big" sacrifices. Expensive jewelry, new appliances, or even a new vehicle are some of the big-ticket items men typically go for. The problem with this type of gifting is that it is sporadic. Letting our intimate partner know they are cared about only once or twice a year is far too infrequent. Special gifts need to happen at least once a month.

The term "special gift" does not mean that our presents need to be something *extraordinary*. What make the gift special, is that it is *out of the ordinary*. Special gifts are a way a couple can break up the routine of their daily lives and let each other know how much he/she is loved. Special gifts should be shared perhaps once a month or even as frequently as once a week. To be more frequent, means special gifts need to be less expensive. A new pair of diamond earrings is not needed every month to keep the relationship alive. What is required is that each person in the relationship goes out and picks up some small item that lets his/her partner know that attention is being focused in his/her direction.

Giving small special presents, like cards, CDs, or DVDs, are ways to display our attention frequently and regularly. If you like the conventional gifts of flowers or a card, remember that the key to love is attention. Therefore, bring as much attention to the gift and the gifting process as possible. Invest energy in finding the card with the perfect expression of your affection. When buying a card, spend time to write out a sentiment that expresses how you feel about your partner. Signing a card "Bob" will not do. Let your partner know what is special about her, why you are thankful to have her in your life.

The same is true for the gift of flowers. Spend time at the florist and pick out an arrangement yourself. If you do not know your spouse's favorite flowers, get blooms that match the colors that are found around the house. Purchasing an already created bouquet at the market is a start, but it does not show a lot of thought or energy.

Back in Chapter 6, we saw that love tends to become lost as the novelty of the relationship wears off. As couples settle into married life, they tend to fall into a routine that takes all the mystery and excitement from the relationship. Gift giving can face the same fate.

~

In one of our therapy sessions, Penny shared that her husband gave her flowers "all the time."

"Yeah, every Friday without fail my husband brings me a bouquet."

Her comment was flat with no sense of excitement. The repetitive nature of his gifts, the same thing on the same day, killed the gift's "specialness," she reported.

~

Vary your presents, both *what* you give and *when* you give them. It is nice to get candy for Valentine's Day, but it is predictable. Unexpected gifts are a more effective way to let our partner know we care. It sends the message, "I am giving this to you for no other reason than because I was thinking of you."

Some women may be thinking that this section is referring to what their partner should be doing. Please understand that these suggestions apply to both sexes. In traditional roles, men are the big givers. As noted above, men typically show their love by giving special gifts. Cultural expectations of women are different. A woman is expected to care for the relationship through service—it is by taking care of all the details of daily living that a wife demonstrates her affection. Thus, women may view service as their only means of giving.

Both individuals need to bring attention through special giving. Men should give special gifts more consistently, while women would be well advised to express their affection through *more* than cleaning and cooking. Both people need to give special gifts, cards, and mementos to each other.

In following chapters, we will discuss the different types of gifts that visual, auditory, and kinesthetic people like best.

Simple Gifts

We all know about attention-seeking behavior, simple gifts are "attention giving" behaviors. Simple gifts are not smaller versions of special gifts. They are small and intimate ways in which we give our partner our regard. Giving is not limited to presents. It includes bringing attention through our actions. Simple gifts demonstrate our care as a part of our daily routine.

The gift object itself is not as important as the thought behind the communication of adoration. For example, just the other day one of Lynda's favorite brushes broke. My going out and buying a new one was a tangible sign that I was paying attention to her needs and wants.

Another simple gift might be to stop at the market to pick up eggs or milk. Simple gifts do not have to cost anything, but they are ways to demonstrate we are remembering our mate. A shoulder rub, a post-it note with a heart drawn on it, or even a word of encouragement—all are examples of simple gifts. These will vary depending on how your partner best receives attention. The point is, whatever we give as our simple gifts should be done every day.

If you were to ask most married couples if they loved one another, the answer is often "yes." But if you then followed up with the question "how?", you would get a blank stare. Gifting is an active way we express and renew our feelings of affection.

Caring

Gifts tangibly communicate our feelings of love to our partner. Yet, we cannot buy love. Learning how to give is important, but couples also need to learn how to nurture the marriage by spending time and serving.

Caring for a garden involves more than simply watering. Weeds need to be pulled, plants are trimmed, and the soil needs to be fertilized. When two people start dating special and simple gifts are ways the pair show affection for one another. Their expression of affection does not stop there. They also go places and do things for one another. These two activities: service and dating, create and maintain a feeling of closeness. Giving expresses our affection, while serving and spending time together develops and sustains the bond between two people.

We care for our relationship through service and dating.

The second means for building a better relationship involves caring for one another. This nurturing phase is broken down into two parts: service and dating.

Service

Service is about doing things for others, taking care of their needs and wants. It is not only a way to show we care. Service, just as importantly, maintains the relationship by renewing our own feelings of love.

It is a mistake to approach service as you would gift giving—as a tangible way to give attention to your partner. Doing for a partner actually benefits us more than it does our partner. Taking care of your partner's needs is not by definition an effective way of expressing love because often the things we do for one another are often not tangible, are frequently repetitive, and are not perceived to be "gifts" by the recipient. The value of service is that it connects *us* to our spouse, but it does not always result in our spouse becoming more connected to us.

For example, getting gas, changing the oil, and rotating the tires are maintenance needs that Lynda's car requires. I know that Lynda appreciates it when I point out the time I take to service her car, but it does not normally cross her mind that my service is a gift. The same is true for the things Lynda does for me. Making a meal involves shopping, cooking, and cleaning. Even though I am grateful for all she does, each part of the process does not stand out in my mind as a gift when I sit down to eat. Much of what we do for one another goes unnoticed. Hence, the real value of service is that it directs and focuses our attention, thereby connecting us to our partner. Giving gifts connects them to us and lets them know we care. Service, on the other hand, connects us to our partner.

The reason our partner does not notice our acts of service is not because he/she does not love us, but because of how attention itself functions. Doing routine tasks for others does not capture their awareness because, as a general rule, attention is drawn to novelty. There is nothing new about doing dishes, so most of the time no one notices.

There is another quality to our attention that does come into play when we care for others. Intensity draws attention. Our awareness is stirred by two things—novelty and energy. In the same way that something new captures our notice, activity also grabs us. A bang, a flash of light, or a tap on the shoulder gets our attention, particularly if it was unexpected. Actively doing something for someone else requires energy. The energy we exert focuses our attention, and our attention creates a sense of connection.

We enjoy watching fireworks, seeing large waterfalls, or attending sporting events and concerts, in part because of the high energy involved in each. Some people always have the TV going in their home or the radio playing in their car because the activity on the screen and the sound from the speakers captures and holds attention. In other words, our attention goes wherever we direct our focus and energy. Service is a way to bring vitality, and thus our regard, to the relationship.

Service is defined as anything that we do for the other person with intention. The more energy and attention we put into a deed, the greater love it will stimulate. When I spend all afternoon shopping with Lynda, if I complain the whole time or bring little to no energy to what we are doing, I will return feeling like it was a waste of a day. By contrast, if I invest myself in the process and bring some enthusiasm to the shopping experience, I come back feeling like we had a mini-date. The activity sustains my focus and in turn draws me closer.

When, in a relationship, we feel distant and disconnected, we cannot wait around for our spouse to make us feel loved. Our feelings need to be our responsibility. Service is one of the ways in which we rekindle the care we have for one another. The effort we put out focuses us on the other person, and that, in turn, sparks our feelings of affection.

Lynda has shared with me that when she does simple tasks such as folding the laundry she will think about each person in the family as she folds and puts away all our clothes. By the time she is done with the load, she feels connected with each member of the family.

The act itself is not where the love occurs. Otherwise, a maid, house cleaner, cook, or busboy would be falling in love with everyone they serve. Love is brought through the amount of attention given to the person who is being served. What the activity does, however, is provide a focal point for our attention, and a way to sustain our regard for long periods of time. The effort we put into something helps hold our focus, and our single-mindedness brings a sense of closeness.

It may take me an hour to wash and detail my wife's car. During the course of that hour I could allow my mind to wander and think about work, to review past conversations, or simply to daydream. If I allow myself to do that, I am just as disconnected at the end of the task as I was before I started, because I did not bring any love-attention to the task. If I use the job to hold my thoughts on Lynda, then my heart feels open and loving before I am done.

The key is that my service must be a free gift. If I expect some kind of response from my spouse, then my focus is actually on getting my needs met. It is appropriate to have someone say "thank you" or to even ask for an acknowledgment if it is not offered. The value of the experience, however, is not contingent on whether he/she notices. For our action to create a mood of love, our attention/service has to be offered freely. Service appears to be something we do for someone else, when in truth, we are the beneficiaries of our actions. If you do something for someone else with the expectation of being rewarded, you will be disappointed. Our acts of kindness need to always be a way to connect, as a means of drawing closer. If what you do for someone does not come as an expression of your love, or a means to create a bond, then do not do it.

Attending to our partner begins by focusing on his or her needs and wants. To paint the back fence because you think it looks bad does not qualify as service. If your partner is unhappy with the way the fence looks and you, paint it for your spouse, that is a loving act.

Doing for others involves meeting their needs. In the same way, going to work and bringing home a paycheck is not service. Our jobs provide for the family, but service needs to be a more direct means of doing something for someone else.

Service softens and serves our heart. Service is valuable to a relationship because it connects us when we are feeling disconnected. When a couple is feeling distant, or when emotions are running high, and there is no reasonableness to be found between them, it may be difficult or impossible to get the two to sit down and discuss their issues because there is no common ground between them.

Typically, when a couple comes into counseling in such a high level of distress, I give them the homework assignment to serve instead of talking *about* the situation. I ask the couple to help each other at least once every day. Their acts of service must be done without the other person's knowledge. The suggestion is to "not let your right hand know what your left hand is doing." By the end of the week, the couple will usually come back and report how much closer they feel toward one another. Once the two have created a foundation of affection, then and only then can they begin to discuss their issues.

Lynda and I do the same thing with our kids. Our favorite consequence for being mean or hurtful to someone in the family is to sentence the offender to serve the person who has been offended. If

Wesley yells at his little brother, his "consequence" might be to pick up the clothes in Trevor's room.

In fact, I suggest that *all* couples should do loving acts for each other at least once a day. That may sound overwhelming, until you consider that we already do something for each other several times every day. We do not necessarily have to go out of our way or do anything special. It requires only that whatever we do should be done with its focus on our partner—do the dishes, vacuum the living room, or perhaps mow the lawn. Just do it with your complete and sincere regard focused on the person you are serving.

The value of service is always greatest when done with our whole and complete attention. One can take the most mundane of tasks, but, when we do it with our complete regard focused on the one we love, that focus will transform the task and our emotional state, as well.

Dating

Our gifts draw our partner closer to us, and our acts of service connect us to our partner. Dating serves yet another purpose—it bonds two people together. Dating is an opportunity for two individuals to begin to form an identity as a couple. The focus of going out together is not to meet our needs or even those of our spouse. The reason that couples should date is to create specific time together for connecting.

Dating ought to be "sacred" time for both people. Sacred means to set aside or to make special. Dating is a time when all the drama of life is set aside and each person brings all of his/her attention to the other person. The more attention we bring, both to the planning and execution of the event, the more effective it can be in re-establishing a bond. It benefits both the relationship and each individual.

My standard suggestion is that a couple should spend a minimum of 5 hours per week bonding. As an ideal, a couple should add a half hour for each year the two are married. This means that a couple who has been married for ten years needs to be spending ten hours every week "dating." That would translate into several evenings a week, or maybe one entire day devoted solely to the two of them. Remember, however, that love is not a function of time, but of attention.

Dinner and a movie is the most popular activity for dating couples, and it is a good example of what does not work when couples normally go out.

~

Terry and Lynn made it a point to go on a date every Friday night. After a few months, the regenerative qualities seemed to fade. The problem rested in their understanding of attention.

Every week, Terry and Lynn would go to their favorite restaurant, then to a flick. Their dialogue during the meal was usually focused on coordinating schedules or deciding on what film to see. Moreover, the loud crowd and public venue did not allow for any deep conversations. Next, the two would move on to the cinema, where they would focus their attention on the screen and not on each other. As you can see, they gained nothing (in relationship terms) from the two or so hours of simply sitting together and watching the film. By the time the couple had gotten home, they had been out for over four hours, but only 15 to 20 minutes might have been spent focusing directly and lovingly on each other.

~

Another aspect of this "habitual" approach is that attention seeks novelty and intensity; it is stimulated by things that are new and exciting, so when Terry and Lynn would go out to the same places and do the same things week after week, the excitement of their dates would predictably wear off, and it all became a part of the "business as usual" in their relationship.

The suggestion I gave them in our sessions together was to mix things up, to create variety and change in their dating life—have pizza in the park and take a long walk.

Responding to this request, the next week Terry and Lynn went out to a video arcade and played games. Their date night was a completely different experience; as a result their relationship felt new and alive.

Talking

Sharing our feelings and asking for our needs are important ways for both people to connect. Most of us understand the value of discussing what we are feeling. This is why the majority of books written to help couples, focus on communication. The emphasis in most of these texts is directed to how you can effectively discuss your issues. In this section, on learning how to love your partner, the focus will instead be on how to get your partner to dialogue with you.

Learn how to speak so your partner will share and listen in a way that he/she will continue to talk.

As a minimum, everyone needs to spend at least 20 minutes every day talking to his/her intimate partner. This means by the time the two go to sleep, 40 minutes of dialogue should have taken place.

This discussion time between the two of you needs to be about non-stressful topics, such as conflicts or disagreements. Also avoid talking about household business like scheduling activities for the kids or letting the other know about your calendar. The intent behind communicating about general topics is to keep the connection between the two of you alive. Hence, stressful or conflicted conversations do not qualify as bonding time.

Instead, talk about each other. Share the events in your day, funny stories about the kids, or your hopes, fears, and dreams. Spend quality time letting your spouse into your world.

These are going to be one-sided conversations, with one person sharing and the other listening. This is not the time to resolve issues.

The more verbal person in the relationship will have no problem sharing for 20 minutes. Problems more often arise in getting your mate to open up and talk. For this reason all the suggestions provided in the segments on speaking with your partner will be directed toward engaging your spouse in a conversation. Each of the next three chapters are chalked full of ideas of how to get a visual, auditory, and kinesthetic person to open up. The ideas will be divided into learning how to speak, and ways to listen that will promote your spouse to want to communicate.

Speaking

One of the fundamental steps in sharing is defining who is going to be the listener and who is going to do the talking. The time to decide, however, is not during the conversation. Consequently, one of the first suggestions I make to couples is that, prior to any discussion, they should clearly establish who is sharing and who is listening, as well as what, exactly, those different roles entail.

When one person is trying to make a point while the other person is resisting, or making his/her own point, what the two are doing is not communication. It is competition. By analogy, in any sport—whether it is basketball, football, or soccer—you can always tell your opponents from your teammates by how they react to you when you have the ball. A teammate will assist you as you work to make your point, but an opponent has a completely different agenda. His/her objective is twofold: to block you and then to move forward to make his/her own point. When we do not help our spouse express his/her ideas, our spouse certainly is not going to help us in making ours, because he/she sees us on an opposing team. In this type of setting, the two people involved are adversaries, not allies.

A few Native American tribes had a custom of using a "talking stick." Sitting around the fire, a group of men would pass a decorated staff among themselves. Whoever was holding the stick commanded the attention of everyone else in the circle. The first thing I ask a couple to do when they are about to begin a discussion is to designate who is going to share and who is going to support.

In my office I use a tissue box in much the same way as a "talking stick." When a couple talks with each other, I ask the person speaking to hold the Kleenex. This signifies that he/she has the floor, and, more importantly, it defines the role of the listener. While the speaker is holding the box the listener may talk, but only to ask questions or to request clarification. The purpose of the tissue box is to signify the direction in which the attention is flowing. The primary obligation of the listener is to provide his/her complete regard. Any comments should be in support of the speaker. Once the person sharing has completed what he/she needs to say, the box is then passed to the partner and the roles are reversed.

The tissue box also serves another purpose; it provides gentle pressure on your partner to share. Nagging never works to promote a conversation. The silence will prompt your partner to engage.

Listening

A general tip: regardless of what type of person is talking, listen as if you were listening to a friend. I call it the "girlfriend mode." The reason girlfriends make such good listeners is because "it is not about them." It is easy for a friend to get behind you when your spouse is being unfair, because you are talking about someone else's mistakes. What makes listening to our partner difficult is that his/her upset is with us. Each of us, if we can ignore of the fact we are being accused of perpetrating a crime, can understand our partner's feelings. The trick to good listening is to not take what the other person is saying personally. Be a "girlfriend" to your husband, or wife, and listen.

Let your partner's upset be what it is. Listen to your spouse's feelings but do not take them on. He/she is sharing feelings. Do not react to what is being discussed, even if it is being touted as fact. Depersonalize the situations and act as if he/she is talking about someone else. Our attention is not on ourselves right now; it is directed toward their feelings. This can be expressed as, "Yeah, I can hear how I hurt your feelings."

When your role is to hear what your spouse has to say, forget yourself and bring him/her all your attention.

Homework: Begin the maintenance program for your marriage. This week, bring your spouse a special gift. Also, set up a date.
Each day, do little, attention-giving behaviors, give simple gifts of your attention, which wordlessly tell that person you care.

How To Proceed

The next three chapters take the topics of giving, caring, and talking, and apply them to the three ways people take in information: visually, auditorily, and kinesthetically.

If your partner is a visual person, then by all means proceed to the next chapter. However, if he/she is auditory, then skip to Chapter 11, and if your spouse is kinesthetic, then Chapter 12 is where you want to go next.

Chapter 10

The Visual Lover

Bringing attention . . .
to a visual person

One of Laura's wedding shower gifts was a new journal. Sharon, the friend who gave it to her, shared how she and her husband, Jake, had used the journal to keep their relationship alive. The diary was kept on the coffee table. The two of them used it to write love notes, expressions of their appreciation, or to share a few words of encouragement. "After writing in it for a while, I would simply see the journal sitting on the table and would begin to feel my love for Jake, as well to feel his love for me."

People often tell newlyweds like Laura that their love will not last. That does not need to be the case. Our love *can* live for a lifetime. What needs to happen is that we must feed those feelings of affection in order to keep them alive. Even the deepest ocean will dry up if it is not replenished. So too our love can become depleted, unless it is continually renewed.

Thus far, we have learned that love and attention are identical and that giving, caring, and talking are the three predominant means through which couples bring each other their regard. We have also seen that not just any kind of attention conveys our affection. For our efforts to be received, they must be channeled in a way that assures our partner's understanding. In giving our attention as a free gift, we must first be mindful of our spouse's style of attending—visual, auditory, or kinesthetic.

The journal story that opens this chapter is an example of how to bring attention visually. This chapter suggests other ideas on how to give, care, and talk to someone who is visually oriented.

The specific ideas for bringing attention are endless. Therefore, the next few pages will not give an exhaustive list of suggestions. Instead, the goal is to identify the general needs of a visual person. Filling in the details and adapting the ideas presented here will be part of your gift of attention.

Gifting

There are two kinds of gifts we bring to our partner: special and simple gifts. Special gifts focus on tangible objects, or presents, while simple gifts are "attention givers", ways we can give our attention to our spouse throughout the day.

Special Gifts

Once you have identified your partner as a visual person, then your gifts need to be visible symbols of your love. Esthetically pleasing presents are what your partner requires. An attractive (versus comfortable) piece of clothing is what will do the trick. Trinkets and accessories that make him/her look good are the kinds of presents visual people appreciate.

The classics all work well with the visual person. Flowers, cards, clothing, and jewelry, are things he/she can see and understand. What is important to remember when giving to a visual person is that your present must be something that can be seen. Pictures of you, the kids, and the family are winners. Artwork, nick knacks, or baubles for the home are also representations of your affection.

If it is still a mystery as to what your partner needs or wants, simply pay attention. In discovering what kinds of gifts your significant other appreciates, be mindful of what he/she sees. Notice what he/she notices. When you are together at the mall, take note of what your spouse looks at, what interests him/her. Then double back after work or after the kids are dropped off for school.

There will be particular stores, brands, and styles that your spouse enjoys. Go through the house, look in your mate's closet, use what is around you as a template for what to get. Often, visual people have some type of collectable that they take pleasure in viewing.

Visual people generally like to read. If this is true for your spouse, notice what authors or what sorts of books he/she savors. Is there an artist or a style of art your spouse admires? If all else fails, include window-shopping as one of the activities on your next date and see what appeals to your partner.

Presentation counts!

To a visual person, presentation is at least half of the gift. When communicating with a visual person give a lot of thought as to how you present it the gift. Wrap the gift, do not simply hand it to your partner still inside the store bag. If your partner gives you gifts that have bows, ribbons, and all the other kinds of cute ornaments on the outside of the package, then make sure your gifts are packaged in the same way.

When wrapping a gift, spend just as much time with the wrapping as you did thinking about what to get. Take a glue stick and lightly dab it on the top of the wrapped present, then dust it slightly with glitter or sparkles. Look for ideas on the Internet or check out a Martha Stewart book on wrapping. Be as creative, and invest as much time as possible into making a wonderful presentation. Attention to the details of presentation is just as much an expression of your love as is the cost of the gift.

Bring attention to how you give the flowers or card. See if you can sneak them into the house and have the flowers arranged nicely in a vase before your spouse sees them. Hide the card in her purse or his jacket; put it on top of his or her pillow with two pieces of chocolate. Be as thoughtful about the way you bring it as you are about what you bring.

As we pointed out earlier, make a real effort to give special gifts at least once per month. Every now and then, of course, a month will have in it an anniversary or birthday. In most months, though, your gift will not commemorate a holiday or a family milestone. Instead, it will simply be a free expression of your affection.

Simple Gifts

Simple gifts are different from special gifts in that they are something you can share with more regularity. Simple gifts can be once-a-week—or even daily—offerings. Naturally, simple gifts need to be modest enough so that they can be given with some frequency. In fact, your offering does not have to be anything you purchase, it involves only finding tangible means for giving your regard.

Written messages are excellent visual cues for communicating your care. Write a love note. Place post-it notes around the house that say, "I love you." One of my clients took the book his spouse was reading, skipped ahead a few pages and wrote in the margin, "I am glad we are together." Even drawing a heart on a steamy mirror expresses your fondness in a visual way. One couple I know has a white board in the kitchen on which they write notes to each other: "Thanks for getting gas for the car" or "You look good today"—short, quick one-liners that take only a few seconds to write.

Even an e-mail may go a long way in delivering the message that your partner is loved, because it lets the loved one know you are thinking about him or her.

When you compliment or write a thank you note to a visual person, use descriptive praise. Although it is perfectly adequate to use expressions like, "You're my best friend." or "Nice job on the kitchen" or "You are a wonderful mother to the kids," what works even better for a visual lover is to describe what you see. It is important for a visual person to know you see what he/she sees.

A visual person processes auditory or written feedback, by creating "mental pictures" of whatever is being discussed. To say "Thank you, you did a nice job" does not create strong visual images for the recipient, but a more detailed and specific description of exactly what you see and what you appreciate about the other person will make a stronger impression and will be better understood. For example, if you compliment your visual partner about his or her parenting skills, spell it out. "Nice distraction. When the kids were fighting earlier, it was impressive to see how you got them to stop by having them work cooperatively on that puzzle." Break down your compliment into specific comments about what you observe. Instead of "You're my best friend," get specific with an observation of the action that gave you that feeling. Such as, "I appreciated you sitting up and listening to my fears about work." The comment, "nice job on the kitchen" may be too general for a visual person. Perhaps something like, "The kitchen looks great, the floors were so clean, the counters were so neat, and all the dishes had been put away. Thank you." The specific description of what you perceived lets your visual partner know you noticed.

~

Jill will tell Kirk, "I love you." Kirk's response is, "Why?"—not because he is being difficult, but because the words alone have no reference, nothing to hang it upon.

If Jill were to say, "I felt loved when you washed the car today." Kirk would know exactly what she meant.

Hence, when you love your visual partner through praise, it lets him/her see what you see.

~

Another simple way to give loving attention to your visual intimate partner is with cues placed around the house.

~

Mike and Francis used a stuffed bear named "Lovey" to bring attention to each other. Every few days, one of them would hide

Lovey in some special place for the other to find. Once, Mike found Lovey in the freezer on top of a container of his favorite ice cream. Another time, Francis discovered Lovey sitting in the driver's seat of her car. Wherever Lovey was placed, it was done with thought and attention to the other person. That little bear became a way for Mike and Francis to provide a visual demonstration of their regard for one another.

⌒

In my personal life, when I am in a playful mood I will look at Lynda as she watches TV, and whenever she looks over at me I will look away as if I was focusing only on the television. Then, when she looks back to the program, I will look at her for a few moments, until she "catches me" again. As annoying as that may sound to some people, it is a visual expression of my attention.

Your attention is intangible, and as long as it remains inside, your partner will not know how much you care. Both special and simple gifts are ways that you can show your affection. When your partner is a visual person, your attention needs to be visually manifested through your gifts.

Visual Caring

Giving gifts lets the other person know he/she is adored, but a relationship needs more than presents to grow. Spending time together and serving the other person's needs are two more vital ways to nurture your relationship. To strengthen a marriage, partners need to spend time taking care of each other's needs as well as hanging out together.

Visual Service

Serving your visual partner means taking care of his/her physical environment. A visual person likes things to be neat, clean, and organized. The home should look nice and tidy. Therefore, by straightening up your spouse's surroundings you may be attending to the visual person's needs. Check this out, of course, to be sure that your partner really appreciates these small gestures. But if you discover that to be the case, remember that whenever you clean the house or make the car look good, you make your visual partner feel loved.

It sounds simple, indeed, but how many times do you not pick up your clothes, not put away your dishes, not fold and hang your towel? If your partner is a visual person and appreciates neatness and order, then these little gestures are wonderful ways to serve. And do not limit your attention to the messes you make. Whenever you find something lying about, put it away.

The key to serving a visual person is to focus on details. The more consideration given to the particulars, the more attention your partner will perceive and the more loved he or she will feel. For example, when you clean off the kitchen table or counters, take an extra moment to assure that the salt and pepper shakers are placed neatly together. In the family room, do not simply stack the magazines, but make sure they are all facing up and that their spines are together. This loving attention to detail always makes a visual person feel happy.

When you take care of how things look you demonstrate that you care about how your partner feels.

If you choose to prepare a meal be conscious and creative about the menu, as well as how it is presented. When you bring your partner a cup of coffee use the nicest cup you can find and then place it on a matching saucer. You also may bring a piece of his/her favorite fruit.

Conversely, when your partner brings you coffee, a gift of service would be to make sure the kitchen gets cleaned up—including putting away all the dishes and clearing the counter.

Once again, be conscious that service needs to be offered as a free gift, with no expectation of appreciation. Do not look for praise—that is not what it is about.

At our house, Lynda and I use chores as a way for our boys to serve the family and as a way to bring attention and love to the household. One of their jobs is to set the table for meals. Children are naturally self-centered. Hence, asking the boys to focus their awareness we are showing them what it means to love others through service. Beyond the basics—china, glasses, silverware, condiments—we ask that they pay particular attention to how the table looks. We encourage them to arrange things neatly and uniformly, perhaps even to cut some flowers for the table. The "chore" of setting the table can become routine and mindless, so asking them to focus on the table becomes a way for them to bring their regard to the family.

In giving service, we serve ourselves. Although we are doing for others, service connects us with those we are caring for. If my spouse was in a coma, she would have no idea about what I was doing, but the act of bathing her, brushing her hair, and reading to her would keep my heart full of love.

Dating Visually

Dating is an important part of caring for a relationship. Spending time together is how we create an identity as a couple. To let the other person know that he/she is a part of the relationship, our partner's desires need to be factored in as plans are made to go out. By this time it should be obvious, but the key to dating a visual lover involves keeping an eye on how things look. When you choose a place to go out as a couple, be aware of your surroundings.

Dining out is the most popular activity couples do when dating, so the view, the ambiance, and the cleanliness of the establishment are probably every bit as important as the meal itself. Select a restaurant that has a panoramic view of the city or overlooks the sea or mountains. If that would stretch your resources too much, look for a place that has "atmosphere" and save the "extra special" location for a very special occasion.

For a more casual evening out, find a restaurant close to home with a particularly nice decor. Tablecloths, wallpaper or murals, clean carpets, and mood lighting make the meal special for a visual person.

Dress well. Be conscious of how you look, because he/she will see it as a reflection of how serious you are about the date. Most likely your visual partner has spent considerable time getting ready, wanting to look his/her best. Your date is not simply being self-indulgent; the underlying reason is to look good for you, to show you that he or she cares about you. Do the same, and present yourself attractively for your partner.

Even on a "home date," when you cannot go out because of a tight budget, or other logistical difficulties, create a date-like environment at home by establishing a nice decor. Bring consideration to how you set the table, use the best china, and silverware. Use matching napkins, tablecloths and place settings. Create a flower arrangement with cut flowers from the garden or the market. Be conscientious to how things look, even down to how you arrange the items on the plate. If all of this is done with love and care, you could order takeout or even pull something out of the freezer—the meal itself will not matter. The presentation will.

Dating activities that stimulate a visual person might include window-shopping, visiting art galleries and museums, or walks in lush natural settings like arboretums or well-kept public parks. If you want to be more active, then go hiking in the woods or along the coast, but make sure wherever you go that there is much to see.

Sex—Making Love Visually

Visual, auditory, and kinesthetic lovers have different ways of expressing and fulfilling their sexual desires. A lover who is primarily visual will not necessarily respond simply to your nakedness, nor will a hasty disrobing and a mad dash to the bed arouse a visual partner. What works is a visually satisfying and stimulating setting, a visually pleasant environment. Pick things up, put away your clothes, make the bed or neatly pull the covers down as if you are in a nice hotel. Light the room with candles or perhaps with a single, low-wattage lamp to give the room a warm glow. Pay attention to the little details that make an environment pleasant and appealing.

Play to the visual lover by making yourself appealing, as well. Wear something attractive, comb your hair; in other words, prepare the occasion as a visual feast. Putting on a striptease show or doing a little exotic dancing may work amazingly well. Yes, it may feel uncomfortable at first, but if you make a game of it and shed your inhibitions for even a few moments, sparks will fly. Above all, spend time looking lovingly at your partner, and give your partner time to look at you.

In moving your visual partner into the mood for love, use descriptive praise, "That gown draws out the color of your eyes." "You have beautiful skin." Draw a picture with words. Emphases what you see and describe the details that please you. "The way you pulled back your hair really shows off your incredible face." The compliment becomes more meaningful by pinpointing the appeal you are seeing and feeling.

Talking

Before discussing how to talk with one another, let me again emphasize that our focus is still upon bringing attention to our partner. Hence, the how-to discussion will emphasize speaking in such a way that our partner will feel heard, and listening so our partner will speak.

Speaking Visually

The old adage, "a picture is worth a thousand words" is true, even when the picture is verbal. Visual people talk in images. Therefore, use metaphors and similes. "Your eyes twinkle like stars." It can be difficult at first to train yourself to use this kind of descriptive language, but a little effort in this direction may have considerable positive effect on your visual partner.

~

Mike is frustrated. He works hard at his job all week, and then finds his weekends filled with "honey-dos" requested by his wife. When he shared his frustration in our session, Windy simply sat and listened. Wendy did not allow herself to get defensive. She instead tried to show support by describing what he was expressing in a simile—a "like" statement.

"It's like being at Disneyland, and you agree to go on all the rides everyone else chooses, thinking at some point it will be your turn. The whole day goes by and you never get to go on the rides you wanted to go on."

"Yeah, that's it exactly. I feel like I haven't picked a ride for awhile." Mike felt heard.

Instead of getting into finger pointing, Wendy wisely drew a picture of what he had said. In doing so, she promoted an exchange of information that kept the two of them communicating rather than correcting.

From that day on, whenever Mike felt burned-out he would simply tell Wendy, "Everyone is pickin' the rides." The phrase became a shortcut, a mutually recognizable metaphor, a quick way to vent his frustration. And since it had begun as Wendy's Disneyland simile, Mike knew she understood. Mike did not like to talk, so if Wendy had spent time asking questions and trying to draw out his feelings, Mike would only have become more frustrated. Mike really wanted validation of his feelings, not a venue to talk out all of his emotions. This is why Wendy's snapshot of the problem worked so well.

~

When your partner has the "tissue box" or whatever it is that signifies he/she has the floor, your job is to assist your partner in making his/her point. By going along with what your mate is stating, you are encouraging him/her to say more. The best way to do that for a visual person is to draw a verbal image of what is being expressed.

It is also helpful to use the visual language that such a person uses. For instance, build your feedback around words like "see," "picture," "look" and other visual words as you give feedback. "I *see* your point." "I can *picture* that." "I can look into that." "I get the picture." "I wasn't looking at it that way before, but now I can see your point." "That's clear." Using words that are familiar to the visual person will help your partner to know that you understand

Listening Visually

A visual person will watch to see if you are listening. A visual person wants, literally, to *see* your response. Your eye contact and your body language will determine for the visual person whether or not the message is getting across. When you make and maintain eye contact with a visual person, you are creating and reinforcing a belief in the other that you are being attentive and that you care about what is being said. It does not matter if you agree or disagree with the point or idea being discussed but it does matter that you are showing your love by being attentive.

If you are not looking at a visual person when he/she is speaking, then, in the opinion of that person, you are not listening. The visual message overrides any verbal expression. You can say, "I hear you", but if you are looking away, the visual person will not feel heard.

Body language during your response or feedback is a strong cue for a visual person. If your body language doesn't agree with what you are saying, then a visual person will likely assume that the visual clues are expressing the correct message. A statement as strong as, "You're right! That is a brilliant idea," will be discounted by your visual partner if you break eye contact, lean back in your chair, fiddle with some item on a nearby table, or scratch your head. *Your body language needs to be in tune with your response.*

This is also where mismatches in relationships occur. Imagine a kinesthetic person who enjoys being comfortable, is stretched out on the sofa or leaning deeply back into a recliner. In walks a visual person who wants to talk about something rather important. As the conversation develops and becomes more emotionally charged, the kinesthetic listener will slouch even more to offset the negative energy. The visual person instantly picks up the shift and interprets it as he/she does not care, or he/she is not listening

A professor who taught one of my undergraduate counseling courses gave me deep insight into this non-verbal communication process. He taught—using the acronym F.A.C.E—how to sit while in session with a client. I am sure it sounds rudimentary, but I have remembered his teaching daily, and it has, without doubt, improved my counseling outcomes. Here is what he said.

"First, the 'F.' Sit *Forward* in your seat, on the edge of the chair, as it were.

"Then, the 'A.' *Align* yourself with the other person by pointing your body directly toward that person.

"The 'C' stands for *Concern*, a certain 'look' you place on your face to imply genuine interest and a caring attitude.

"And finally, 'E.' Keep good *Eye Contact*."

This system is simple, yet effective.

Use facial expressions and body movements in an "authentic" way. Nod your head when you agree or to indicate that you understand. Raise your eyebrows once your partner has made a point (whether you agree with that point or not), change your facial gestures as you listen. This small, but sensitive process will give your partner visual cues that you got the message.

Whether you are giving, caring, talking with or listening to your visual lover, always remember the old phrase, "I'll believe it when I see it." *Make your gift of attention something that is seen.*

Homework: On the assumption that you have been successful in doing the monthly, weekly and daily behaviors described in Chapter 9, this assignment is to now refine your skills by applying the ideas offered here on how to give, care, and date your visual lover.

Pick one section from giving, caring and talking, and play with the suggestions provided. The following week select another area. Keep up the behaviors you started in the first week. By the third week you should be bringing your full regard to your partner through all three means, giving, caring, and talking.

Chapter 11

The Auditory Lover

Bringing attention . . .
to an auditory person

"Mmma."

When no one else is around, and the house is quiet, Lynda or I will make a "kissing" sound. Lynda, being the more auditory person, started doing it years ago. I have picked it up, and began doing it back as one way to speak her language. Our kissing noise conveys, "I am thinking of you, I acknowledge you." Most importantly the smooch sound carries the message that I am bringing you my attention, thus letting the other know, "I love you." It is done when one of us leaves the room, or after a long silence, from reading or watching TV. We do it also as a signal that Lynda or I are going to bed, and a means of saying "good night." It is my method for giving auditory attention to Lynda.

The basic need for a couple to give, care, and talk to each other remains the same for all relationships. What varies is how that is accomplished. Depending on the style in which your partner best receives attention will change how that is done.

These next few pages will outline how to give both special and simple gifts of attention to an auditory person. We will also discuss how to maintain a relationship through serving and dating someone who is auditory. The last section will share the secrets of how to talk to an auditory audience.

Gifting

In expressing our affection, we give gifts like flowers, cards, or jewelry. That is all well and good, and it works particularly well if your intimate partner is a visual person. But an auditory person needs something more (and sometimes, something else) because an auditory person needs to *hear* as well as *see* your love.

Special Gifts

Our gifts to an auditory lover should, if nothing else, create a pleasant listening experience. An auditory person would appreciate a new stereo, tickets to a concert, live theater, or similar special gifts. Make a trip to the music store and pick up a tape or CD of his/her favorite artist or environmental sounds. Wind chimes or a music box are both nice. The key is to think in terms of *sounds*.

Auditory gifts may be more than music. They might include books on tape, inspirational or motivational audio or video presentations, informational, educational, or entertaining tapes. Another example: take in a free community workshop or lecture on the arts, psychology, or whatever topic interests your partner.

Be aware of which radio stations, music, and musicians your partner appreciates. By being conscious of those likes and dislikes you will not have to reinvent the wheel. It is the time and attention that you put into finding the right gift that will make it special.

If you still cannot figure out what to select as a special gift, ask. Auditory people like to express themselves. A conversation about what he/she enjoys doing, listening to, or receiving will be a pleasant treat in and of itself.

However, do not ask about an event directly, "So what do you want for your birthday?" Ask in a more conversational style, "Who is your favorite artist these days?" "What's going on with Richard Crawford? Does he have any concerts coming up?"

Other gift ideas may involve the absence of sound. Spending the weekend away—without children—works, too, as long as the place is quiet and serene. Lodging at a national park or creating an escape at a quaint bed and breakfast could be ideal for the auditory partner.

Lynda has a strong sensitivity to noise, so one of the gifts she enjoys frequently is a new pair of earplugs. She will wear out a pair every three to four weeks, so keeping her well stocked lets her know she is loved.

Simple Gifts

A simple way you can give to your auditory-type lover is by providing praise and acknowledgment. Your auditory lover needs to hear you verbally appreciating what he/she does, and orally recognizing what he/she says. "That pot roast was very good", is a polite response after a meal. Keep up the compliments. Say, "thank you." The verbal appreciation goes a long way with an auditory person.

Too often, however, our praise is only in response to something the other person has done for us. Our regard needs to be given more freely. For our comments to be felt as loving, they must be unconditional. Like love itself, our praise works best when it is unattached to any event or activity.

"I appreciate how hard you work for the family."

"Honey, you do a great job taking care of the kids."

Feed your relationship by daily verbalizing what you appreciate about your partner. Share unsolicited praise or give compliments for no apparent reason. These kinds of remarks let the other person know you are thinking in a loving way.

Do not tell your auditory partner that you love him or her—describe why.

~

Jack comes into the living room where his wife, an auditory person named Helen, is picking up her e-mail.

"You know, you are really beautiful," says Jack.

He need not say anymore, for it is spontaneous remarks like this one that win the heart of an auditory lover.

~

Another point of awareness when you are addressing an auditory partner is inflection. Think not only about what you want to say, but also consider how you wish to say it—your tone, inflection, pacing and pauses. If your words come out in a monotone, or if you express the same thoughts and ideas in the same way over and over, even the inspiring message "I love you" is heard in the same way as "I am going to work now," it will come across almost as if nothing at all had been said.

Bring energy to your voice, and some vitality and enthusiasm to what you are conveying. The time and effort you put into saying just the right thing in just the right way translates even the very simple sentence "I love you" into a golden chain of magic words. That "loving feeling" can also be heard in expressions like "You handle the kids with an artful blend of strength and care." As we know, attention is stimulated by originality and "oomph." Bring these two elements together and you will make your partner feel deeply loved.

The other gift we can bring to an auditory person is that of a loving, considered response.

Lynda occasionally tells me that even though I think I have answered her, I may not really have said anything at all. It is an unending source of wonder to me because—since I am a kinesthetic person—*the very act of thinking about a response actually, to me, feels like a response.* She will ask about making tacos for dinner, for instance. I will think it is fine but I will not respond verbally. I am honestly unaware that I have not actually said the words, "That's fine by me."

Obviously, my failure to say something is not intended to be a turning away from her, but that is how she perceives it. Lynda needs to hear what I am thinking. Part of my ongoing, daily simple gift to her is to make an effort to verbalize my reactions, to respond to her bids for attention.

Your partner's bids are often comments about the weather, bits of news, or inquiries about your day. Your partner simply wants is a brief reply that indicates that you are listening and that you care.

Another way to give is to make bids of your own. Check in with the other person throughout the day. If you work away from home, call on the phone once or twice a day, just to say hello. And at home, keep the loving contact going with little remarks like, "Hey, sweetie" as you pass one another in the hall or make eye contact across a room. These seemingly insignificant comments provide important acknowledgments of your partner's presence and value.

Auditory Caring

To fix the garbage disposal or to make a nice meal for an auditory person may not be considered direct service by that person. Bringing attention to your actions by expressing them in words may be the key to reaching that partner who lives in an auditory world. Your successful strategy will be to pay attention to how things sound, how you and your partner talk with one another, and how the general acoustical environment supports and nurtures your relationship with one another.

Service

An auditory person needs to converse. Thus, one way to serve your spouse is to provide opportunities for conversation, for each of you to express yourselves. In this context, serving may simply involve sitting and listening.

Set aside 15 to 20 minutes every day to touch base with your partner in non-stressful dialogues. Make time to chitchat about the day's events and catch up with the events of each other's lives. It is human nature to seek out pleasure and to avoid pain. Therefore, make these interludes pleasing conversations. Keep the dialogue light and comfortable. Bringing up difficult topics during this sort of conversation may serve your own needs, but it will almost certainly not serve your partner. Bring up your frustration and hurts at another time and place. It does not matter that you solve the world's problems between you when you have these conversations. Often, just talking about what happened on the way to the market may be enough for the auditory person to create an internal feeling of being cared for.

If you cannot find a topic to discuss without tensions being raised, experiment with using the time to read to one another. When an auditory person is involved, the need is for calm auditory input, so if one or both parties do not know what to say for 20 minutes, reading may provide a pleasant, non-threatening environment in which to connect. Take turns, with one person reading for ten minutes and then the other

Not only does the auditory person need to speak, but also there is a need to hear. Hearing your voice fulfills part of your partner's auditory need; reading aloud fulfills the other, even when the material is neutral. It can be helpful, though to read to one another about a topic that is problematic for the relationship. When the problem between two people revolves around the children, try reading a book on parenting. If difficulties arise around sex, one suggestion would be to read a good sex manual. Read something about finances if the issues between you are about money.

There is a certain safety in this, by the way, because an "outsider's" view of a given issue remains neutral even though the practical issue between two people may be highly charged with emotions. And there is no need to discuss the material after you have read it, because it is not important for the two of you to agree or to reach consensus. The objective is simply to spend time together and to serve the auditory person's need for a verbal exchange. By sharing together a book about a touchy topic you may create interest and motivation, but do not get involved in a battling over whose way is the "right" way.

"Following-up" is another way to care for your spouse's need to talk. By checking in with your partner about something that was discussed earlier in the week, you let him/she know you have been paying attention.

For example, on the day before Randy was to give a presentation at work, he shared his anxieties with Amy. The following evening Amy asked him about how the presentation went.

If the challenge is an ongoing problem like sibling rivalry, follow up with questions about how things are going. Make a mental note to keep asking even if your partner has not raised the issue in several days.

Check in and see how what was discussed yesterday went today.

Another item to consider when making time to talk is the environment in which the conversation occurs. For example, I love to munch on snack foods. A good bag of chips or even a handful of dried cereal is "my kind of crunch." Unfortunately, the sound of my eating drives Lynda crazy. She will often simply leave the room to avoid becoming irritated. This obviously denies both of us the social connection we need with each other. One way I serve Lynda is by being aware of the sounds around us. When we are together to share our day, I make sure that I am not eating. I do not try to start a conversation when the kids are running around making noise. Before we talk I turn the TV off, shut down the computer, and put down whatever project I am working on. Serving an auditory lover involves creating a quiet atmosphere as well as establishing an opportunity to share about your lives.

Dating

It should come as no surprise that when you are planning a date for your auditory lover you need to be sensitive to the sounds in the environment. Dining out is a favorite activity for most couples. Therefore, pick a restaurant that is quiet. Find a place without screaming children or a loud bar area. When you arrive, make sure you sit away from the kitchen. The ambiance or quality of the food is secondary to the acoustics.

During the summer, many cities have evening concerts in the park. Bring a picnic basket and a blanket and make the whole experience enjoyable.

Some dining establishments have quiet music playing, feature a piano player, or even provide live entertainment. An auditory person appreciates these refreshing places.

Dinner theaters put on a play or a musical performance while the guests eat. Other establishments have their guests get involved with the production. The waiters and waitresses double as actors, and they put on a murder mystery while you dine. The fun of these kinds of places is figuring out who did it before you finish dessert. These venues appeal to the auditory person.

Wherever you go or whatever you do, the most important objective of the date for your auditory lover will be the pleasant exchange. What makes a perfect night out for an auditory person is the opportunity it creates to sit and talk. In this context the two aspects of caring for the relationship blend together. It will not be the quality of the meal that will define the success of the evening, but the quality and quantity of the conversation.

Sex—Making Love Audibly

An auditory person needs feedback when it comes to physical contact. Some people are silent lovers. Making love without a word or a sound will satisfy some people. That will not work well with an auditory person. What these kinds of lovers need is praise, compliments, and verbal stimulation. If you are a visual or a kinesthetic person, describe what you enjoy. When you get excited about something sexy your partner is wearing, let it be known. If you enjoy how your lover touches you, or how it feels to touch your lover, let your mate know. Moan a little. Say, "Oh yes!" now and again. These expressions of excitement work wonders with an auditory person and will probably make the encounter even more pleasurable for both of you.

Around Patrick and Lynn's house the rule is that they have to avoid any conversation about money if the two of them are planning an intimate occasion later that evening. In fact, sex usually does not happen on the nights Patrick is paying the bills. According to Lynn, that is because . . . "Patrick gets a tone, a sharp edge to his voice, when he gets stressed."

Even if the tension and frustration in his voice has nothing to do with Lynn or anything she has done, his tone shuts her down. Her ability to become sexually stimulated increases or decreases with the qualities of the sounds around her. Hence, Patrick needs to learn that good sex in his relationship with Lynn starts with the tone of his voice.

When making love to an auditory person, create a pleasant mood or atmosphere—turn on some sexy music, get a recording of ocean waves or rain forest sounds or a babbling brook. The sound environment will create the mood you want, and it will also demonstrate that you are paying attention to his/her needs. The more your partner can feel that you are focusing on pleasing him/her, the more he/she will be interested in pleasuring you.

Talking

Speaking Audibly

Lynda likes to razz me about the fact that when I come home the decibel level in the house increases dramatically. As I come up the drive, I typically blast my horn to announce my arrival. The boys begin yelling for "daddy," and I return their cries by calling out their names. Growling, I then attack them with hugs and tickles. The room becomes filled with squeals and laughter as we wrestle to the floor. I play louder, I even talk louder than Lynda. Whatever I do seems loud. Until it was pointed out to me, I did not realize it because I am not an auditory person.

Because I am naturally louder than Lynda, I get accused of "yelling." Of course, this upsets me, and the upset raises the volume even more. Lynda, in turn, shuts down. The issue is not that I am shouting, rather, it is that I am not being sensitive to how I come across.

We (Lynda and I) already know that there are no good guys or bad guys. My style is no better or worse than Lynda's, but if I want to get into a dialogue with her I need to speak in a way that will cause her to open up, not shut down.

In speaking to an auditory person, you need to be sensitive to what will stimulate a conversation and what will kill it. For this type of person, the full value of the conversation is not only in what you say but also in how you say it. The volume, tone of voice, and pace of your speech all affect an auditory person.

When you engage in a conversation with your partner, set up the situation to encourage success. Silence any outside distractions like TV, radio, power tools, or even running water. If you are a visual or kinesthetic person, be aware that you have a tendency to be active while talking. If you are cooking or doing the dishes while you are striking up a conversation, the auditory person will feel drowned out by all the extra noise and activity.

Listening Audibly

Auditory people like feedback from their audience. It helps them to feel "heard." Statements like "I *hear* you" or "that *sounds* good" use auditory words that let the speaker know you understand in the same way in which he or she understands.

"I *feel* bad for you" is a kinesthetic response. "I can *see* what you're saying" is a visual reply. Even though they carry the same meaning as "I hear you," the impact may not be as effective with an auditory person because the language being used is not consistent with auditory vocabulary. The message, then, is: provide feedback an auditory person in the style and with the vocabulary that he or she uses.

The technique called "Active Listening" works well with an auditory partner. Active listening involves repeating back what you hear the other person saying, as a way to verify that you got the message.

Sally shares with Bob, "I didn't pick up the kids on time, because I went to the bank to get my check cashed and the lines were so long I couldn't get out of there on time."

Bob could make eye contact, and nod his head at the appropriate times, but if he does not say something back, Sally still will not be sure if she was heard. "It sounds like the lines at the bank really messed up your schedule." By rephrasing what Sally said, Bob let her know he understood.

The active listening exercise is not magic; there is no hidden power in the technique. Like any of the exercises suggested in this book, the effectiveness of this activity comes in the level of attention that you bring to it. When I first work with a couple in my office and introduce the exercise, it generally goes over exceptionally well.

The weeks that follow often bring a diminished return. Unfortunately, when the couple returns home and uses it several times, the novelty may wear off, and both of them will probably begin to use mechanical phrases or speak with a monotone voice. "I hear you, but..." Because there is no real attention brought to his/her partner, the exercise will not continue to be effective.

Put some thought and energy into your Active Listening.

The secret to truly effective listening is found in both using the correct approach and giving full attention to the action. The active listening technique is a means for each member of a couple to shift attention by changing the focus of response away from his or her own feelings and on to the partner's issues by creating an accurate feedback loop. For an auditory partner, this kind of verbal feedback validates his/her feelings.

Homework: *The Active Listening Exercise*. On a daily basis, serve your spouse by sitting down and talking for 15 to 20 minutes. Pick a time after the kids are in bed and the house is quiet—but not so late that either one of you is too tired to talk.

At the end of each thought your partner shares, practice repeating back in your own words what you heard your partner express. If he or she corrects you, listen to what changes, then try again repeating it back.

Remember, your response will be even more effective if you use auditory language ("I hear that...").

Chapter 12

The Physical Lover

Bringing attention . . . to a kinesthetic person

Sudden Change

Carlos and Kelly came into a counseling session in my office complaining about their "communication problems."

~

"I try to talk with him," Kelly began, "but all I hear is how tired he is. Well, I work as hard as he does, so I don't understand why he can't talk."

Carlos lashed out, exclaiming, "She expects everyone to be like her! It's not as easy for me to just dive into a conversation. It takes work to talk, and when she gets home I don't have the energy."

~

Once I coaxed them past the blame game using some of the techniques we learned earlier, I discovered this was a recent change for the two of them. Carlos used to talk at length with Kelly about her day, but now he seems to "check out," plopping down in front of the TV to watch the news.

What was different for them now? Whereas until recently Carlos would arrive home about an hour before Kelly, he now got home at about the same time as she did. It turned out that he still wanted to do what he had always done—to take an uninterrupted hour or so to unwind before Kelly would arrive and they would talk over dinner. But the new circumstances made that impossible, and Carlos never had a chance to recharge.

Carlos was a kinesthetic person, deeply involved in feelings and emotions, while Kelly was an auditory person. When the two of them came home at the same time, it became a clash over which partner's needs were going to be met. He was looking for some down time to recover from his work stress, while she was also looking to decompress from her day, but what she needed was to talk. Once the battle began, neither of them cared much about what the other person wanted because they became stuck in whose way was the right way.

The solution was simple. I asked Kelly to delay her desire to connect for the first hour, to let Carlos relax and recharge. Once he had enjoyed his down time, Carlos was to spend the next hour talking with Kelly. The system worked marvelously, just as it had previously.

Gifting

In discussing how to give to a kinesthetic person, creature comforts always dominate. The kinesthetic person is acutely aware of the way life in the moment is being physically experienced. For a partner dealing with a kinesthetic other, it is vital to be in tune with how things feel to that kinesthetic other. This knowledge and understanding will make it possible—even quite easy—to figure out what to give to him or her.

A kinesthetic person

enjoys how things feel.

Special Gifts

When deciding what to give to a kinesthetic lover, think of things that will provide comfort or offer physical stimulation. Therefore, anything that can be touched or handled will potentially interest a kinesthetic person.

Activities and adventures, such as a small day trip to the mountains or the shore, can fulfill the kinesthetic's need to experience life. Walking in the sunshine, running hands through the sand on a beach, feeling the texture of tree bark, smelling flower blossoms in the spring—these are the experiences that are meaningful to the kinesthetic person.

If he/she likes to be around crowds, the gift may be a trip to an amusement park. If your partner is a true extrovert, being around other people will enliven and revitalize him/her. These special trips may be for a day or a weekend. What is important, is the opportunity to get out and be active.

For a kinesthetic partner, select gifts of clothes based on how they feel or gifts of food based on how they taste. More than a pretty bow or a neat package, a comfortable pair of sweats or a few nice sweets will meet the need to be nurtured.

Make a nice meal of all your kinesthetic's favorite foods. And, since kinesthetic people love comfort, serve the meal in a comfort-filled environment. Breakfast in bed, for instance, is a wonderful experience for a kinesthetic.

If you are married to a kinesthetic person it may, at times, be difficult to meet all his/her needs to be touched and to experience sensate events. So, you might want to give a special gift of a trip to a day spa, or treat your lover to a professional massage.

If you are a highly visual or auditory person and find it hard to select something from a kinesthetic perspective, try sampling gifts with your eyes closed. With clothing, get a strong sense of how the material will feel as opposed to how it looks. With food, concentrate on its taste and smell and less on how it looks.

When in doubt, ask your partner for help. One couple, having great trouble satisfying the kinesthetic partner, created a "wish list" for him. Once he spelled out what kinds of gifts appealed to him, she asked him to prioritize the list like a David Letterman "Top Ten" list. By numbering the items from least essential (10) to most essential (1), she not only got an idea of what he wanted but also the relative importance of that particular item.

Simple Giving

Simple gifts for a kinesthetic lover consist simply of providing daily physical contact. Touch is how a kinesthetic person best receives your personal regard and feels your love.

Simple gestures go a long way with a kinesthetic. For instance, when you are watching the TV news together, give your spouse a foot massage or a gentle backrub. Hold hands when you are walking, driving, or just "hanging out." Rest your head in your spouse's lap as you read this chapter. Touch as frequently as possible. A light kiss on the head when your partner is working at the computer will send a powerful message of love. A brief caress any time, in almost any situation, transmits love and translates as caring to a kinesthetic person. In bed, sex is not all it is about for a kinesthetic—it is about contact. So, snuggle up when the two of you are lying together in bed. By the way, contact is a two-way street. A kinesthetic partner will very much enjoy giving *you* a rub down, so do not hesitate to ask.

There is no better way to make meaningful contact than to give a "conscious hug." Holding each other intentionally and consciously is very different from a "typical" embrace, which looks something like this: you put your arms around one another, pulling each other close for a moment. Maybe your partner gives you a few quick pats, or you may give a kiss on the cheek—and it is over. These quick embraces are quite satisfactory when shared with a friend, but they will not stir passion in your marriage.

Next time you give your spouse a hug, take your partner in your arms, but this time pull your lover close, creating full-body contact. Start with head and shoulder contact, then draw your partner's entire body to yours, bringing your torsos, your hips, and even your knees together. Breathe in—deeply—together, then relax—deeply—into one another's arms. As you release your breath, drop your shoulders, melt into the hug and allow yourself to conform your body to your partner's body. Then take a second breath and send loving energy to your mate.

If any uncomfortable feelings come up, allow yourself to use your breath to release the negative emotions. *Resist the temptation to pat your partner.* That distraction is a way of releasing tension by breaking up the intensity of the moment. Instead, use your breathing to let go of any hurt/fear/anger and to bring you into close, direct contact with the moment.

Physical Caring

Caring for your relationship means stimulating your own feelings of affection and developing a greater sense of closeness as a couple. Service and dating, as discussed earlier, fulfill these two objectives by directing attention differently from the way in which gift giving did.

Physical Service

In the context of intimate relationships, when one talks about serving, most people think first about having sex. For a kinesthetic person, making love is definitely a part of the equation, but serving goes far beyond sex. Serving involves giving attention in such a way that it connects you to your spouse and vice versa. Kinesthetics want to "feel good." A "Norman Rockwell" interpretation of a kinesthetic person being cared for would show a man sitting comfortably in his recliner and being given his favorite slippers, the TV remote and a bag of chips.

Think about how you might use the concept of loving service to create such a scene for your kinesthetic partner. The key word here is "comfort." It could be that you encourage your mate to cuddle up in bed with a good book, to hang out in a hot tub or take a leisurely, warm bath—any restful, regenerative activity that will provide the "creature comforts" will service those kinesthetic desires.

Consider giving your partner 20 to 30 minutes to unwind at the end of their day at the office—or with the children. As your kinesthetic partner's needs are being met with a comfortable respite, your act of service might then be to take care of preparing dinner, or dealing with the children, or perhaps just spending the time relaxing with your mate—no conversation, just relaxation. Part of being attentive, of course, is noticing whether your partner enjoys time alone or prefers company.

In my own relationship, it is clear to me that Lynda needs downtime—but that she would prefer my company. She is primarily an auditory lover, but she has a secondary kinesthetic style. This means that sometimes she needs time to unwind (kinesthetic), but she is even happier when she can sit down, unwind, and talk (auditory). The only thing that Lynda loves more than sitting and reading is to have me sitting and reading with her.

I am a kinesthetic personality, but I am the active type. My physical needs are met by being on the go. Hence, sitting quietly and hanging with Lynda is a somewhat difficult gift of service for me to give; it is a passive act and does not require a lot of energy. Yet, in order to give the gift fully I need to repress my need to get up and water the garden, and this is difficult for someone like me, who is always on the go.

There are active and passive kinesthetics.

As we can see in the above example, the needs of a kinesthetic person may actually go in either of two directions—active (me) or inactive (Lynda). Some kinesthetic people are into ease and comfort, while others are into accomplishments and activities. A note of caution here: be aware of whether your partner is always "on the go" because it is a part of kinesthetic enjoyment or whether it is simply that the work at hand needs doing—now.

My personal ideal of being served would be to have Lynda spend time with me in the backyard as I trim the hedges or clean the pool. A glass of cold lemonade would be nice, but I would be just as happy to have her hang out with me as I work in the yard. She would not need to rake the leaves or even hold the trash bag open. It would be pleasant simply to have some company.

Remember, whether you are sitting with your physical lover (passively keeping company as he/she works), or if you are actively serving (as your kinesthetic person relaxes), the key to service is to focus on the other person and to let your actions help direct your regard toward your spouse. The more freely you give your attention to your spouse the stronger your feelings of affection will become.

Dating Physically

The "dives" of the world exist because of kinesthetic people. When a restaurant is referred to as a "dive" it usually means it is a run down, greasy little hole-in-the-wall, and its only redeeming value is its great food.

Ambiance, soft music, romantic lighting and décor, a nice view— none of these matter to a physical lover when it comes to restaurant selection. What he/she desires is good food. When it is time to take your intimate kinesthetic out to dinner, choose a place that will cater to your partner's physical body. For example, overstuffed booths and large portions of really tasty food may turn out to be essential criteria for a nice evening out. If your selection of restaurants ends in a need to compromise, remember that creature comfort comes first for a physical lover.

~

One evening Kelly took Taylor to a nice Italian restaurant. He is auditory and Taylor is kinesthetic, so Kelly selected a restaurant that had excellent food (Taylor's kinesthetic creature comfort needs) *and* a piano player (Kelly's auditory characteristic).

Typically, couples race in and out because they have an agenda to keep, perhaps the 7:30 showing at the local theater. Kelly and Taylor, though, simply took their time and enjoyed each other's company, sometimes talking and sometimes silently and appreciatively listening to the piano. The needs of both were being met in this auditory/kinetic setting.

~

Action and activity are what some kinesthetic people crave. If that is the case, perhaps a restaurant that not only serves food but also has dancing would be a good choice. When the agenda is to spend some energetic time together, look for a swap meet, a County fair, a church fair, an amusement park, a ballgame, or even a local park where you can just walk or toss a Frisbee back and forth.

These action-packed evenings may or may not provide an opportunity for intimate conversation, but the physical activity will stimulate and connect you and your partner.

Sex—Making Kinesthetic Love

What a kinesthetic lover may lack in communication skills is usually compensated for by an innate ability to make love. Kinesthetic people, by definition, are very "touchy-feely." They not only enjoy being touched, but they also have the gift of touch—they know what works, what stimulates, what enlivens a partner. The language of the caress is native to the kinesthetic, and learning how to caress a mate is quick and easy.

When making love with your kinesthetic partner, create as much variation as possible. Change the locations and times of your lovemaking. Try it in the kitchen, bathroom, shower, or pool. Instead of always having intercourse in bed on Sunday evening between 9 and 10 p.m., indulge in a "quickie" before work or on some Saturday afternoon after the chores and errands are all done. This variety will ignite things between you because the "newness" of each encounter will appeal to the kinesthetic's desire for new and different experiential sensations.

Physical lovers also enjoy using an assortment of different positions. When you are making love with your kinesthetic lover, emphasize physical closeness. Skin to skin contact, long periods of foreplay, and gentle caressing make intimate occasions more satisfying for the physical partner. Introducing body oils—or, for the more visual lover, body paints—creates opportunities for physical play. Spend time touching each other's arms, or stroking his/her legs. The more physical touching, the better. Make the bed with soft, silky sheets. Wearing silk pajamas increases the tactile sense of pleasure.

Talking

Speaking Physically

Sheldon and Janet are opposites: he is quiet type, she is more verbal. Shel will do anything for Jan, but what she wants most is to have a quiet conversation. This is uncomfortable for him, he does not know what to say.

As I get to know Shel a little better during our sessions, I discover that he enjoys working on the treadmill prior to getting ready to go to bed. I suggest to Jan that she wait until Shel has started his walk on the treadmill, then approach him and ask about how his day went. The activity of working out satisfies Shel's kinesthetic sense, thus allowing him to focus on their conversation. The release of physical activity also tends to offset any discomfort he might feel when he has to open up and share about himself.

Physical people need to be active as they speak. There is body involvement even in their conversation. They will often speak with their hands, and they generally display dynamic facial expressions when they talk.

To help a kinesthetic to relax and open up in a conversation, provide something to "play with." Give your mate sculpting clay or play dough. A pencil or pen and a doodling pad may do the trick. In my office, I provide rope or steel puzzles for kinesthetic clients to tinker with as we talk.

Be active as you converse.

Instead of sitting and facing each other, take a walk in the park. Many of the best conversations between Lynda and me occur while we are walking down the beach near our home.

By the way, for a kinesthetic person, holding hands as you walk down the shore creates an enormous sense of connection. This, coupled with just enough activity to satisfy the kinesthetic's needs for action, may create even more room for two people to talk seriously. Driving together can also provide an environment that will help your partner to share.

Every evening, as Mike is on the way home from the office gives Kendra a call from his car. The two spend a few moments talking about their day and sharing about the kids. The activity of driving helps Michael to be attentive, while Kendra is able to sit and talk quietly on the phone. Since she is a visual person, sitting still and talking is important as she unwinds from the day. For Mike, on the other hand, after listening to people all day long, it is helpful to be doing the action of driving as they share.

When you have a conversation with your active lover, you might ask for a light massage. Let your partner rub your feet, or let your lover massage the stress out of your shoulders as you discuss your day or upset. Have a conversation while your partner is doing the dishes or cleaning the counters. By discussing an issue while your kinesthetic mate is fixing a light switch you are getting your needs met to talk while also getting help with taking care of things around the house. Physical activity aids your mate in staying focused and attentive. Common tasks like making dinner together or folding the laundry provide enough stimulation for a physical lover to share thoughts and feelings quite openly.

Find effortless tasks to do together that will keep your partner's focus as you talk. Washing windows or sweeping the driveway are simple enough activities so that one could easily carry on a conversation while continuing to work. Sit down and work a puzzle together, play a board game, break out a deck of cards. Let your mate fiddle with a pencil or tinker with a pen if it helps him or her to stay focused.

It goes without saying (but I will say it anyway) that some tasks demand too much concentration to allow for effective conversation. Working on the computer and responding to e-mail, for instance, require rather intense involvement and therefore do not lend themselves to listening or talking. Although it might seem that watching television or a movie would permit a conversation, such is not the case. TV powerfully steals our attention. Even the mute button does not fix the problem, as long as that screen is on, the attention of the viewer is stolen. The program (or even the commercial!) does not matter. TV claims the entire focus of most viewers. And talk radio is not far behind. Most listeners are concentrating on the broadcast content and cannot divide their attention to include a "live" conversation. So be discriminating in choosing what activities to attempt to interrupt with a conversation. Select repetitive tasks that stimulate, but avoid tasks so intense that they absorb all of the available attentiveness.

Listening Physically

Kinesthetic people require a physical a reward for talking. That reinforcement is contact. A pat on the back, a squeeze of the hand, a gentle rubbing of the leg—all create a sense of pleasure and, in turn, support a continuing conversation. A light touch between shoulder and elbow is a strong yet subtle nonverbal way of saying, "Yes I understand, and I want to hear more."

To get your physical lover to feel heard, and hopefully want to continue a conversation, reward with touch, but also be aware of your body language. A kinesthetic person is more aware of your body's communication than that of your words. So, send signals that let him or her know you are interested.

Standing close enough to touch the other party in a conversation this will also serves to disarm conflict. Vulnerability and conflict are opposites. The less vulnerable one is, the easier it is to argue with the other person, create distance, yell, and become upset. When you are dressed in a suit of armor you are ready for war. When you are naked, fighting is the last thing on your mind. By sitting close, holding hands, touching your partner's leg as he/she talks, you not only let your partner know you are listening, but the closeness keeps the conversation from becoming confrontational.

When you respond, speak the kinesthetic person's language. Use words that convey sensations or feelings. Comments like "I know how you feel" or "I bet that *hurt* terribly" incorporate words the physical lover can relate to. It is not that a kinesthetic actually has a better sense of touch or a greater sensitivity to emotions than, say, a visual person might have. But the kinesthetic's awareness of sensation is more responsively approached when "sympathetic" words are used.

To say "I can *see* that" to a kinesthetic person communicates that you are processing the information differently (*visually*), thus the kinesthetic speaker may believe that you do not understand what he or she is sharing.

Homework: Practice, Practice, Practice. Your assignment for this chapter will be to implement the talking tips for your physical lover.

Set aside 15-20 minutes per day to talk to your partner. Make sure you are making physical contact, or that he/she is engaged in some routine task that can easily be interrupted.

For the moment, put your point of view and opinions aside as you simply listen.

Do a lot of head nods and other gestures of support (pats on his/her leg or arm) as your spouse shares about their day.

Section Three Continued

REINFORCE
The Practice of Love^{SM}

Part Two of the Practice of Love
Loving Our Self

In this, the second part of The Practice of Love, couples will discover how to love themselves.

Self-care will consist of learning to communicate what we are feeling, thinking, and needing without causing Right Fights.

Chapter 13

Love Thy Neighbor As Thy Self

Bringing attention . . . to our selves

Prior to asking for Lynda's hand, I approached her father, Jack, to request his permission. He accepted, of course, but he insisted that I hear and take to heart a bit of advice—a truism that *his* father had given him before Jack's marriage many years ago.

"Marriage is a 50/50 deal, but it always feels like you are giving 90% and your spouse is giving 10%."

Just as his father had tried to advise him, my soon-to-be-father-in-law was attempting to prepare me for the reality of married life. Specifically, he was letting me know that there is no perfect exchange of love.

Jack wanted to let me know that marriage often feels out of balance, that there are times when we are, indeed, giving much more than we get. He was not disparaging marriage, but he was letting me know in very simple language, that the seamless give-and-take of love—the romantic image of "perfection" that brings two people together—does not last on its own. Jack's serious intent was to encourage me to continue to bring love to my marriage even when I might not feel loved in return, to urge me to give unconditionally.

His comment was accurate—at least insofar as the feeling of giving more than one gets is concerned. But after nearly two decades of experiencing my own marriage, I take exception to his solution.

He was correct in saying that it often feels as though we are giving much more attention than we are getting back from our partner. The answer, however, is not to "suck it up" and keep on giving. Nor is, *to stop loving,* the way out. We need to learn to attend to our own needs, as well. The solution for each of us lies in our learning to bring attention to ourselves, not just in how to engage solely for our partner's consideration.

The old adage, "It is more blessed to give than to receive" is well taken, I will admit, but to emphasize giving over receiving is a formula for failure.

The previous section of the Practice of Love, *Loving Others,* was focused on how we can bring love to the relationship by directing our attention to our intimate partner. But the work does not end there. We also need to feel loved.

The Law of Love

The Bible relates a story of someone asking Jesus what was the most important of all His laws. Jesus answered, "…to love God with all your heart, mind, and soul. And the second law is like the first; love your neighbor as yourself. Upon these two commandments, depend all the laws and the prophets."[ix]

The second principle brought forth in this well-known biblical quotation is what I refer to as *the law of love.* It is our obligation to bring attention to one another as we bring attention to ourselves.

The word "as" has three definitions, all of which apply. The first definition of "as" means to do something in the *same way* you would do something else. "As" also means to do something at the *same time,* and the third meaning refers to a *similar degree.*

Hence, the law is asking us *to bring as much attention to ourselves—* meaning *in the same way, at the same moment, and in the same proportion* as *we do to our significant other.*

The high failure rate of marriages today is because most couples fail to fulfill this law. It is easy to understand that failure to love our spouse will kill the relationship, but a more difficult concept is contained in the notion that failure to love ourselves will produce the same result. This statement is not meant to have a moralistic flavor. The "law" is simply *a description of the way things operate.*

For example, if a man understands the principles behind the science of aerodynamics, he can create and design a pair of wings, strap them on, jump off a building, and glide safely to the ground. If he fails to understand one aerodynamic principle—called "lift"—then the laws of gravity will go to work and that man will meet with grave consequences (perhaps both literally and figuratively).

In the same way, the law of love is an explanation of how relationships function. It does not tell us "what to do," like a parent to a child. The law of love tells us there are certain principles, operating independently and always acting in the same way, and that if we follow those principles properly we will produce a living, growing relationship.

A couple needs to understand the nature of how love functions in order for their relationship to succeed. If both people do not comprehend the need for self-love as well as for the love of the other person, the relationship will fail.

Both People Must Fulfill the Law

Most relationships exist in what I call "a state of quasi-balance," in which one partner does an excellent job of self-loving (usually the male), while the other is devoted to loving others (generally the female).

Men in western societies do not often seem to have problems asking for—or doing—what they want. Conditioned by our patriarchal western societal norms, men can easily and naturally bring attention to themselves with little or no guilt or inner conflict. A man can spend all week away on business and then have no shame about going golfing with friends on Saturday. While men do a good job of looking out for their wants, often they can be blind to the needs of their significant others.

Moreover, when asked to serve the needs of others, a man's attention is typically not given as a "free" gift, but instead comes with something of an "attitude." And if a "typical" male has to do something he does not want to do, he may do so grudgingly, with lots of huffing and puffing and rolling of the eyes. He may give, but often it will happen on his time schedule or will be done in his own way. Pushed to do what he does not want to do a man's gift of attention is often not free—it comes with a price tag in the form of a selfish or self-serving motive, usually expressed as "What's in it for me?"

By contrast, women do an excellent job at caring for the needs of their spouses and their families. Women have the uncanny ability to bring attention to myriad different issues and needs simultaneously. They love to give, for that is how they have been brought up. Moreover, women generally believe that their needs will be taken care of by their significant others without their having to ask for such consideration.

As a general rule, women do not express their own desires directly through words or gestures. They intrinsically believe in the "love exchange." Because they so demonstrably take care of others, they expect that someone will love them in return and will magically take care of all their needs. Because of this obviously "cloudy" belief system women fail to bring attention to themselves. It is not that they do not like to receive attention, they just do not believe that they need to ask someone else for the attention they need.

Have you ever heard (or said), "If I have to ask, then I don't want it." Some women believe that to ask for something detracts from or invalidates that which they are requesting. For a woman to ask directly for her needs to be taken care of may stir within her a resentment stemming from her belief that she should not have to request satisfaction so directly.

Women unconscious understanding that for attention to be experienced as love it must be a free gift. Hence, if your spouse does something for you because you asked, then his act of service is not a true gift of love. The fact that you had to ask him to take out the trash negates any possibility that his efforts can be an expression of affection. If he had done it without being told, that would have been a better proof of his love. By asking, you will get the trash taken out, but you will not realize your more important need, to be loved.

Therefore, a woman may not ask at all. Then, after waiting to see if her mate is paying attention, she will eventually do it herself and will carry the disappointment back into the relationship, sometimes in the form of a grudge that will grow and grow, magnifying with each similar experience.

To be sure, not all women are unconditional givers and not all men are self-serving takers. In fact, at times the roles are reversed. And it is not simply gender that determines the differences in outlook, action or response. In gay and lesbian relationships, while the genders are the same these polarities continue to cause problems. In same-sex relationships it may be the role-based expectations rather than some hard-wired or education-based belief system that accentuate the differences.

It is my conviction that the issue is not that one gender is better than another or even that there are insurmountable gender differences caused by either genetics or conditioning. I believe that love fails directly—and only—as the result of one or both parties not fulfilling the law of love. For a marriage to be healthy, *both parties* need to fulfill *both sides* of the law.

How?

The most satisfying way to share who we are and what we need—to love ourselves as we love others—is *to communicate in ways that each of us and both of us can understand, agree with, approve of, and act upon.*

Regardless of whether you or your partner are auditory, visual or kinesthetic, communicating is the most effective way to channel attention your way. The style of our conversation should change based on how the other person best takes in information, but the need to draw attention to ourselves remains the same. Talking about ourselves is the best way to get our partner's attention, to let him/her know what we are thinking and feeling, or to express what you need or want, for we all know from experience that the old system of silently loving and *hoping* that love will be returned generally brings us only resentment stemming from our unfulfilled expectations.

It is important to realize, though, that when we *do* care for ourselves and *do* "communicate," we may also create conflict. Sharing our emotions openly and requesting that our desires and needs be met may cause our partner to resent us because of an erroneous assumption (on the part of our partner) that he or she "should have known" what it is we want. Expressing ourselves, at times, can generate more tension than love. Asking our partner to do the simplest task, like picking up dry cleaning, can stimulate opposition, not harmony. The question is: How do express self-love and make clear our needs without creating difficult problems in the relationship?

Real Communication

Paradoxically, it is only when I talk about myself that my spouse is able to hear me clearly. I can share anything—pain, fear, disappointment, frustrations, and even my hopes and desires—if, and only if, all my attention and regard comes from within, and is centered upon myself. By talking only about me I assure that the conversation will emphasize *what is wrong* rather than *who is wrong*, which makes it possible for my spouse to listen freely and without defensiveness.

This opens up possibilities for change. The moment the topic of my conversation shifts from "me" to "her," the risk of judgment and opinion appears, my spouse is likely to move into a defensive stance and the conversation will almost certainly lose its balance and degenerate into a contest rather than a discussion.

To communicate well is

a most effective way to love yourself.

Remember, there is a difference between communicating and correcting. There are several styles to any conversation. Each is distinguished by the focus, goal, and level of emotional upset. When couples are truly communicating they are calmly focusing only upon their individual selves, sharing personal emotions and desires with the singular goal of assuring that the other person fully understands what is being said.

Our conversations, then, are not a means to an end; they are not a way to get the love we want. Each effective conversation is actually a self-loving act.

Here is an example from my case files.

~

Tim, Wendy and I had just sat down to start our session. As I so often do, I began with chitchat about current events in their lives.

Tim shared that he had to attend a meeting after our session that evening.

Wendy reacted strongly, surprised to hear that he needed to go back to work.

Tim instantly became frustrated. "She never remembers what I say. This happens all the time. I tell her things and she does not listen."

Of course, Wendy lashed out, "How am I supposed to remember everything you have to do?" Then, turning to me as if I was to decide who was right and who was wrong, she continued, "Besides, half the time when he tells me these things we are in bed and I am barely awake."

What had gone wrong? Tim's attention quickly collapsed as he became upset, and he began trying to "correct" Wendy's behavior. Because his attention was no longer on himself, Wendy was unable to hear him clearly and instead went on the attack herself. Tim did not communicate his feelings. He corrected her forgetfulness.

Breaking into their conflict, I asked Tim if he would work with me for a moment, and I asked Wendy to sit quietly and observe. They both agreed to my requests. I had Tim turn toward me and talk—with me and only with me—about his upset.

"I understand that it irritates you when she forgets things," I began. "But help me appreciate why you take it so personally. What if she was taking some medication that caused short term memory problems ... would your feelings be the same?"

Tim replied, "No. I feel that she does it on purpose."

"Why would she do that?" I pressed him to dig deeper.

Without a moment's hesitation, Tim responded, "She has selective hearing. She hears what she wants to, then ignores what she thinks is unimportant."

I clarified. "So you get mad when she forgets, because it means that what you said was unimportant."

"Yeah!", Tim responded enthusiastically, as if some light had come on in his head. "I feel like anything I say carries no weight with her."

"That's great you see that, but let's dig even deeper." The focus was still on her behavior. Tim needed to get to a place where he was exclusively looking at his own thoughts and feelings. "What you say has no weight with her. Tell me why that bothers you."

Tim raised his left eyebrow as he looked at me intently. I could only guess that the question sounded so obvious that he was curious as to why I had asked it. As I sat waiting for a reply, he could see I was not going to retract my request. He slowly looked away from me, formulating an answer.

"I feel as though I'm not important. It makes me feel that what I do, or say has no relevance. That's it. I don't feel important." Tim had a twinge of surprise in his voice, as if he was shocked at how personal the issue really was.

Our quick discussion not only clarified what Tim was feeling, but it also helped in calming his upset. The more we talked about his emotions, the more relaxed he became. These two things—clarification and calming—would not have occurred if Tim had not redirected his regard upon himself. He freed his own attention by giving himself some love.

Now that Tim was clearer and calmer, I directed him to bring some attention to Wendy. Turning toward his wife, he took her hand and made eye contact. While the two were touching, I asked them both to breathe deeply, releasing any stress or upset as they exhaled. After a moment or two, I asked Tim to share with Wendy three things he loved about her.

"I love what a good mother you are. I am always amazed at how much you do with the kids, taking care of homework, and getting them to all their activities. I love the way you take care of the house. You do a great job keeping our home clean and making all the meals. I know it's not easy taking care of all the family, and you do it all with such grace. As his final remark he blurted out, "And I think you're beautiful. After all these years together you are prettier now than when we first met."

That last remark was the clincher. In addition to saying that he loved her for all the things she did for him and the family, Tim let Wendy know he loved her as a person. Immediately, I could see her start to brighten as her cheeks flushed with color. Wendy relaxed and a smile came across her face as she moved from a *protective* into a *connective* attitude.

After a quiet moment during which the couple sat, still looking at each other, I asked Tim to go back to their earlier discussion and to again share his feelings with Wendy.

"When you don't listen, it feels like you don't care about me." Spontaneously, Tim went on to express how as a child he was often neglected. "Being the youngest, I felt like no one ever heard me. I was 'cute little Timmy', but no one took me seriously." He went on for several more minutes, sharing his frustration about not being heard as a kid.

Wendy was more supportive this time. "Oh, I never knew why that bothered you so." She then followed up with a sincere apology. "I am sorry. I don't do it to upset you. It is not about you at all. People at work are always getting mad at me for not listening. But I will try harder."

~

Clinically, there were four steps to their process in this encounter. The first two stages of the conversation re-directed Tim's attention to himself by allowing him to discharge some of his upset by discussing his problem with someone other than his wife. The outcome of that conversation also provided him with an understanding of what needed to be shared. Becoming calm and clear regarding his perceptions required Tim to direct his regard to himself.

In the last two stages, Tim shifted his awareness to Wendy. Through touch, eye contact, and a few kind words, Tim re-established rapport and set the stage to express his insights. His confession of why he was bothered was a free gift, something he shared with no expectations.

Here is the paradox again: Tim, by directing his regard solely to his own issues, created an environment in which Wendy was able to hear what he had to say. His attention to Wendy, then, was free of any demands. Tim's dual attention, his ability to love his wife *at the same time as he loved himself*, made all the difference. Bringing attention to Wendy, and at the same time focusing on expressing (out of self-love) what bothered him, enabled Tim to discuss his feelings successfully.

As couples, we need to stop using our conversations as a duel for attention. Instead, we need to bring dual attention to the conversation—to our partners as well as ourselves.

The Four "Cs"

These four segments, which Tim and Wendy went through, are what I call the four "Cs":

❖ **Calming**

❖ **Clarifying**

❖ **Connecting**

❖ **Confessing**

To understand how and why these steps work, go back and recall "The Fight That Never Ends" in Chapter 4.

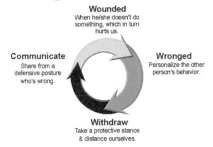

The Fight That Never Ends

Wounded
When he/she doesn't do something, which in turn hurts us.

Communicate
Share from a defensive posture who's wrong.

Wronged
Personalize the other person's behavior.

Withdraw
Take a protective stance & distance ourselves.

A fight usually starts with pain. We feel wounded by something our partner has done or said. The emotional pain, or charge, is then amplified by the belief that we have been wronged. Quickly moving into a protective space, we withdraw. Our disconnection is intended to protect us until we right the wrong we felt.

Once we have attempted to correct our spouse's "mistake," we watch and wait for any signs of change in attitude or actions. When our partner (predictably) resists being told that he/she was wrong, we feel wounded again and our emotional charge increases. The looping conflict will then continue with another round.

The Four 'C's interrupt this cycle at every turn.

To have a normal conversation we need to be in a normal state of mind. Pain, sorrow, and anger stimulate our bodies to move into a fight-or-flight response. Instincts prepare us either to run or to stand and defend ourselves. Therefore, the first step is to *Calm* yourself and decrease the emotional charge.

Before you discuss anything, recognize and take control of (responsibility for) the neurological and biochemical changes your body will experience. Do not look to your partner to feel better yourself. Afterall, it is your partner who has hurt or upset you in the first place. It is up to you to spend a few minutes, or even days, getting your feelings in check before addressing the issue directly.

Next, own your issues. *Clarify* what it was that bothered or hurt you. Somewhere, somehow, you personalized the wound you received from your partner and you saw yourself as being wronged. That perception then increased the emotional charge you were feeling. By discovering how your own thoughts are adding to the problem, you will be better able to take responsibility and thus control your pain.

More likely than not, what you do or say in these situations ties into some pain you have experienced in—or as a result of—your past relationships. The old hurts we carry can magnify the present pain we feel, which then leaves the impression that our partner has hurt us much more than was actually the case. You will need time, to look inside yourself, to separate out what part of the pain is your partner's and what part you are carrying from the past.

We can own our "stuff" and be cool about what we have to say, but if we move into a self-protective posture our partner will move there as well, thus preserving—and perhaps even increasing—the emotional distance between us. Withdrawal and disconnection is all part of the protective posture we take after being hurt.

This work differs from traditional marital counseling because it emphasizes *connecting prior to communicating*. Recalling that emotions can serve to protect us or to connect us, it is clear that when we are hurt, our natural response is most likely to withdraw emotionally, leaving us unable to effectively address the person who hurt us.

By consciously *Connecting*—the third step—we are able to work against the impulse to withdraw and so begin normalizing the relationship. Being connected before any conversation begins helps us to say what we need to say while also putting our partner in a good frame of mind to hear us.

Confession is the final step. I use the term *confessing* rather than *communicating* because it better captures what is taking place when we share our upset. Even if my pain, hurt, or anger may have been triggered by someone else, to confess my feelings demonstrates that I am taking responsibility for these emotions.

In confessing my thoughts and emotions, I am sharing them as a *free gift*, with no strings. It would be nice if my partner would change behavior as well, but that is not the purpose for my sharing. My confessions are expressions of who I am, and the act of confession provides a way of letting my spouse more truly and deeply know me. *It is how I stay current in the relationship.*

There is no more waiting for a response, because I have already brought attention to myself through calming down and by clarifying my feelings. I am no longer setting myself up to be wounded and thus to need to repeat the cycle once again.

In a way, this is much like talking with a trusted friend. In such conversations, I do not need the other person to make my life better. It is simply nice to be able to talk with someone about my life and have that person really listen. Perhaps the notion of looking upon intimate communication in exactly this way—a communication with a trusted friend—is yet another key to creating the harmony we really want in our primary relationship.

The ability to fulfill the law of love—to bring dual attention—defines real communication. Said another way, communication will succeed when both members of a couple are able to fulfill the law of love and bring simultaneous, appropriate attention to both participants. If either partner withdraws attention from the other, thus restructuring the communication into a demand to be loved, the communication will most certainly fail.

The final solution to all Right Fights, then, is to be able to love one's self as well as to love one's partner.

Homework: Begin to practice using the 4 "C"s. Pick an issue that you want to communicate. Spend some time calming yourself. Scream out all your frustrations while taking a long drive, go exercise, call a few friends . . . do whatever you need to blow off steam. Once you have settled down, process what it is about your partner's behavior that you have taken personally. Yes, something inappropriate was done or said, but the real question is: "Why do you feel hurt?" After you have settled down and have clarified your issue, re-direct your regard and allow yourself to get close to your spouse. Using the skills you learned in the last section on loving your partner, create a connection. Finally, confess your feelings and begin to share why you were irritated by the issue.

Chapter 14

Calming

Moving out of the protective posture

Lunch

Mornings are a bit crazy around our house. Lynda and I are usually stretched to our limits (both physically and emotionally) getting the boys and ourselves ready for the day.

One morning's timing was particularly tight. My clients were scheduled back to back, so if I did not make a lunch and bring it to the office I would not eat all day. That morning, however, Lynda also had a need—she wanted to talk.

To this day, I have no idea what it was we were talking about, but I remember clearly that it was not going well. Fifteen minutes into the conversation I had to leave, and we parted with the issue still unresolved and both of us still angry. It seemed as though neither of us would get our needs met. Lynda was frustrated because she was not feeling heard, and I was annoyed that I had not been able to pack a lunch and so would be fasting.

When I got to work I tried to push away my own marital problems and address those of the couples in my office. As the day progressed, it became increasingly difficult for me to forget my issues. I found that my bodily hunger fed my feelings of resentment.

At about 12:30, Lynda showed up with our two small boys—and a lunch! My heart melted. The anger and frustration I held from our earlier clash vanished in an instant.

Even though this situation occurred several years ago, I still remember her comment. "I wanted to do this for you as much as for me." Lynda was feeling as angry as I was. Part of her motivation to make my lunch came from a need to release her upset. She knew by serving me in some way, her emotions would be calmed. What Lynda did that day was to love me as she loved herself. She brought me attention, but in doing so she released her anger. Her kind act freed up her energy and attention, thus making her available to connect.

To love ourselves we need to communicate our feelings. Often, though, at the times we really need to talk we are the least available— emotionally—to do so, because the strong feelings that we want to express stand in the way of open communication.

Decreasing Our Charge and Freeing Our Attention

Two elements distinguish true communication from the corrective or combative styles. First, the words we speak must be free of negative energy. Second, what we express must be spoken without demands or intent to hurt. To speak "in love" requires that our words be like our attention: a free gift.

The moment you believe you have been hurt by someone you love, your body experiences a series of changes that prevent you from being close. In fact, they drive you away from your partner. Couples do not just need to learn to "play nice" or try to watch their tone. What needs to happen is for individuals to calm themselves so they can come to their conversation in a connected space.

No one—not even your partner—cares what you feel unless he or she *feels how you care*. When your audience senses that their feelings and ideas are valued, they will listen and value your thoughts and emotions. The reverse is also true. When you come to a conversation disconnected from your spouse, your spouse will disconnect from what you have to say.

The problem here is that the strong emotions you seek to express tend to place you in a protective stance. This guarded position disengages you and thereby prevents you from being able to effectively share your pain. Powerful feelings produce an emotional, as well as a physiological shift in disposition.

The change in your affect is the result of a collapse of your attention upon your upset. Your feelings focus you on yourself while leaving you disconnected from your spouse.

Emotions are energy in motion.

John Bradshaw, author of *Healing the Shame That Binds You*, describes our emotions as "energy in motion." If this is true, then your strong feelings, even if they are not being outwardly expressed, will direct your attention inward, toward your feelings, leaving little room for attention to your partner and your partner's needs. Because attention is attracted to energy, the weight of our emotions directs our regard to our issues, and therefore leaves our attention unavailable to focus on our partner.

This shift in awareness is not only emotional but also physical. Regardless of whether or not the danger is real, the brain thinks that you are under attack and your body instantly undergoes both neurological and chemical transformations. The physiological and psychological shifts influencing the nervous system tell you to create space between yourself and the source of your pain.

Once the "fight or flight" response has been triggered, the words you say and the tone you use will be dictated by your physiology. Your words will either have a distant and detached quality to them, or they will be delivered in a hostile or biting tone. With attention fixed on your own wounds and your changing body chemistry moving you away from your partner, or pushing your partner away, there is no way that the two of you can have a productive conversation.

Instead of going to your partner to try and resolve the issue or express upset, first spend time releasing these feelings. Rather than

191

trying to talk with your partner in the midst of your hurt or anger in the hopes that the other person will relieve you of your upset, first change your negative charge.

Before any productive discussion takes place, couples should get their emotional state of arousal down below a 3 on a scale of 10. The body's chemistry has been altered, and before you can engage in any kind of sane conversation you need to restore your right minds by returning your physiology to a place of connection.

Traditional Ways to Deal with Our Emotional Charge

The mutually exclusive quality of the connective and protective postures means that it is impossible to be intimate and defensive at the same moment. This fact can also be turned around to work to our advantage. The way our nervous systems are built, we cannot be anxious and relaxed at the same time. Stress reduction programs exploit this fact by teaching people to shut down their anxieties by using breathing techniques or other meditative exercises.

Lynda, at times, will laugh at me because when we talk I often sit and breathe deeply as I listen. Concentrating on my breathing is a way in which I prevent myself from becoming irritated. It is my way of not becoming emotionally "charged" as she shares about her feelings. It also works well to decrease my experience of negative emotions.

I use a technique called Diaphragmatic Breathing and find it to be a very good way to calm yourself in any situation. Here is a summary of how to do it.

Diaphragmatic Breathing

First, check to see if you are breathing correctly. Place one hand over your belly button and the other hand on your chest. The hand on the chest should be positioned so that your thumb is on one side of the collarbone and your index finger on the other. With one hand up high and the other resting down low, notice which hand rises and falls as you take your next breathe. If you are breathing from your diaphragm, the hand on your abdomen will move while the hand on your chest will stay perfectly still.

If you are a visual learner, imagine a balloon inside your stomach. Each time you take a breath, see the balloon filling with air and expanding. As the breath is released, tighten your stomach muscles until the abdomen is completely flat. Taking in another breath, relax your stomach muscles, allow your abdomen to rise, and imagine inflating the balloon. Then flatten your stomach as you exhale and again squish the balloon.

Repeat this imagery for three sets of ten breaths. Between each set stop and stare at a spot on the floor and clear your mind. It is impossible to "work" at relaxing. A hyper focus can create more stress than it relieves, so be easy on yourself as you are first learning.

If you are a kinesthetic learner, imagine breathing from the bottom of your feet. As you breathe in and out, pretend that your legs are two long straws from which you draw the breath up and then release it back down. Feel an imaginary opening at the bottom of each foot, through which you can breathe in the air and draw it up through your legs and into your abdomen. As you release your breath, feel the energy moving back down and going out through your feet. Once again, take in a breath, allow the air to move up to your stomach, and, as you exhale, notice the air moving back down your legs. Breathing this way—from the bottom of your feet—keeps your breath low and slow.

If you are an auditory learner, use "self talk" as you breathe. As you inhale, silently tell yourself, "My breath is deep and relaxing." When you release the breath, recite the phrase, "I am calm and in control." Again, go through the cycle, breathing in the phrase, "My breath is deep and relaxing," and exhaling the words, "I am calm and in control."

Regardless of the method you choose to use, recline when you first try it. Since almost everyone breathes more naturally when sleeping, lying back helps your body to do what it was designed to do, particularly while you are learning these techniques.

Continue to use your hands to monitor your airflow. To make sure the breathing stays exclusively in your abdomen, keep one hand on your chest, the other over your bellybutton.

Take a few minutes right now to learn what works for you. Spend perhaps ten minutes practicing Diaphragmatic Breathing. Use whichever of these three procedures you like. Do not be discouraged if it takes time to master, You will be consciously controlling abdominal muscles you are not used to manipulating. But in doing this exercise you will be acting in concert with the way your body is physiologically built to breathe, and the method will soon become more natural and easy to do.

If your emotions are running high, perhaps you cannot talk about your problems to the person with whom you are upset. Perhaps, then, expressing your emotions first to a neutral third party may work well for you as a means for reducing your tension. Sometimes this might be a friend or family member, but assure yourself in advance of your confidant's neutrality. The advantage of talking with someone else is that you may be able to free your feelings without running the risk of adding to an already heightened emotional state by trying to communicate with your partner in an inappropriate way or at an inappropriate time.

Processing your feelings with a psychotherapist may prove to be even better. Not only will you be able to share in a safe, confidential environment, but also a trained professional will provide informed, honest feedback about your own behavior. Conversing with a counselor may also provide a reliable way to identify the issues behind your upset. You are more likely to discover how your experiences and thought patterns form your feelings as you talk with a trained counselor than you would be when talking with a friend.

If you are not interested in "airing your dirty laundry" to other people, then try writing as an alternative. When you think about highly charged issues your mind may tend to loop over and over the same material, thus keeping you agitated and distressed. Writing has a beginning and an end. It forces us to follow an idea all the way to its conclusion. The empty lines on the page beg for us to dig a little deeper. Journal writing helps many people to work off steam by externalizing feelings onto paper. Or, by writing a letter you never send you may be able at least to clarify what is bothering you.

Talking with someone will appeal to those who process input auditorily, while writing is a more visual activity. If you are a kinesthetic person, get physical. Take a walk, go on a run, or perhaps go to the gym. Remember, emotions are "energy in motion." Therefore, by becoming active you will dissipate your feelings and relieve tension through exertion.

One final suggestion: let time dissolve some of the tension. A good guide for couples is to let 24 hours pass before confronting an issue. When one or both of you are extremely upset over a particular situation, try agreeing to let go of it for a while—take a "time out," just as parents do with their agitated children. Feelings are very fluid and can change quickly from one moment to the next. By allowing a full day to pass before confronting the situation, each partner in a marriage may better distinguish the emotions that need to be addressed from those that are simply the result of a bad mood. If you are still feeling hurt a day later, your negative feelings will certainly need to be addressed, but the discussion will take place free from upsets that steer couples off course.

Love-Based Ways to Deal with Our Emotional Charge

There is a reinforcing cycle between energy, emotions, and attention. High emotions hold our regard, and our concentration tends to strengthen our feelings. This is good when the feelings and energies are positive, but in the face of negative situations those same qualities tend to perpetuate our difficulties.

If I am afraid of flying, the more time I spend focusing on my fears the stronger my anxieties become. Attention creates a bond between me and whatever I dwell upon. And the same is true for you. Concentrating excessively on your anger, hurt, and sorrow will make you more angry, hurt, and sorrowful.

It is a misconception that to focus on unhappiness will make us happy. It is true that we all need to release our emotions, and on occasion that means we must bring attention to our reactive moods. However, continuing to focus on our feelings does not *eliminate* the feelings. In fact, our focus tends to keep those feelings alive. We need to shift our attention to prevent negative emotions from being exacerbated.

Service reverses negative energy.

Love is not only the *ideal*, but it is the *only* means for creating healthy communication. The traditional approaches to problem solving and conflict resolution—such as writing or talking—have been effective because they direct our attention toward our feelings as a way of releasing upset.

Love-based solutions, though, will take us in a different direction; they will shift our attention away from our agitation and direct it toward our spouse.

Service, one of the love-based solutions we have been examining, is an excellent way to work against your own physiology because the energy and effort expended in doing for others will force you to refocus your regard. The story about Lynda making me a lunch was an example of shifting feelings by redirecting her energy and attention.

My brother Matt was a short-term missionary. His assignment was set up in such a way that he was paired with a companion, another missionary. His companion turned out to be rude, selfish, and anything but missionary-like. Shortly after the two began working together, Matt's companion broke his leg, and Matt had to take care of his companion's every need. For the next six weeks, Matt made his meals, washed his clothes and took care of all the chores for both of them. By the time his companion was back on his feet, the two of them had become strong friends. Serving his companion in such an intense manner had softened Matt's heart such that he was able to see past his partner's shortcomings. His companion, on the other hand, responded to Matt's loving attention in such a way as to overcome any natural tendencies toward rudeness and inconsideration. Both learned the value of service in a relationship.

In doing for others, attention is redirected from the self and focused towards the other, thereby reinforcing the emotional connection. Diverting our awareness through service replaces the mood of unlove with that of love.

Do not let your service become mindless. The reason Matt's efforts to care for his companion, were so effective in connecting the two young missionaries, was because the novelty of the circumstance held the awareness of both parties. In a long-term relationship like marriage, after doing hundreds of loads of laundry, preparing thousands of meals, or mowing the lawn countless times, there is a risk—no, a likelihood— that these tasks will have become mundane. For service to effectively change our hearts we need to continually hold the other person in the forefront of our consciousness.

Acts of kindness, in themselves, are meaningless as agents for producing change unless they divert our attention from ourselves, and our upset, and redirect it toward our partner. For that to occur we need to remain mindful as we serve of the one we are serving,

The appearance is that when anger, hurt, or frustration is particularly severe, contact with an intimate partner seems only to perpetuate our plight. For example, when a couple's emotional charge is high—between 8 and 10—to continue a "conversation" would only further the mutually felt negative feelings.

In these situations, it is more effective to take a break and calm down. And what better way to fill the downtime than to do a kind act for your partner? I have discovered in my practice that the more negative the emotions we are feeling, the more effective service can be at neutralizing our disdain.

At yet another level, prayer and meditation can also be powerful tools in transforming your lives and your relationship. These terms sound religious, so if you do not hold a concept called God, think of prayer and meditation as forms of attention. The essence of prayer is that it is a way of directing regard toward another person or toward an outcome.

We are what we meditate upon. Allowing your mind to reflect continuously on negative feelings and thoughts will produce more negative outcomes. The reverse is also true. When you focus on the positive, you will manifest more positive outcomes. Remembering our blessings reinforces our pleasure. Thus, prayer and meditation are positive ways to redirect the mind and refocus thoughts in a constructive manner.

When the emotional charge is so intense that it is difficult to be around a person without snapping or being irritated, the *one-minute meditation* is another way to give attention without getting physically close.

In Chapter 5, *What Is Love*, it was suggested that you focus on your intimate partner for one minute, three times a day. Take the first 15 seconds to clear your mind of negativity. Use your diaphragmatic breathing to release all your feelings of hurt, sorrow, and anger. Then visualize (or look at a picture of) your partner—or whomever you are upset with—for the next 15 seconds. Continue to breathe deeply as you hold their image in your mind. After picturing them, imagine touching them, and then being touched. If any ill thoughts or feelings arise, breathe them away. In the final quarter of the minute, continually breathe in their name, and as you exhale, say to yourself, "I love you."

For those who need to be a bit more active, write a gratitude list. The fact that our connective and protective states are mutually exclusive makes it difficult to stay upset with someone when we are focusing on their positive traits. When you are feeling disgruntled, sit down and write out a list of five reasons you are thankful to have the other person in your life. Having to find five new qualities that you are grateful for forces your mind to look for the positive in the other person instead of dwelling on the behaviors that make you unhappy.

In fact, these little "gratitude lists" can become a form of meditation in and of themselves. Save them and every once in a while review them—daily add to them—particularly in moments when you are experiencing frustration share a few items with your partner.

Pain is a powerful motivator. Generally, couples try to avoid issues that lead to a fight, but mounting agitation often drives an issue to the surface. The problem with allowing pain to be the driving force in a conversation is that in those painful moments you and your partner are not close, and therefore your conversation goes nowhere. Your conversation is based in conflict. It is important, then, that when we speak we are calm.

However, there is a downside to being composed. Being forcibly self-controlled takes away the motivation to talk openly. Being calm will prevent a conversation from going badly. However, absent the unwelcome—but necessary—discomfort of an emotional charge, issues may go unaddressed. As a result, the conflict will remain unresolved. After we take a few breaths, and then pray for our partner, the emotional pressure is relieved. We often tend to want to let sleeping dogs lie. Press on! Do not simply drop the topics that caused your distress. Sharing those feelings will bring you both closer together.

Before you actually dialogue with your spouse you will need to spend time bringing attention to yourself and understanding in more depth what lies at the core of your conflicts.

Homework: You need to learn to walk before you can run. Do not wait until you find yourself in a protective place to practice calming down. Spend time this week mastering diaphragmatic breathing.

Set aside 10 to 15 minutes every day breathing and relaxing. Lie back and use your hands (one over your chest, the other over your belly) to make sure you are keeping your breath low and slow.

Chapter 15

Clarifying

Focusing on what's wrong

Double Standards

"Wes doesn't use the same rules with his three kids as we do with my two boys." Barbara and Wes have come into counseling to discuss a problem they are having with blending their two families. "We have house rules for the children that we both agree upon and enforce, but when his three come to visit, Wes acts like the rules don't exist."

Wes chimes in, "It's different because my boys don't live with us so we can't ground them."

"You can put them in time out." Barbara's tone is more corrective than suggestive.

"It's not the same" Wes replies. "Your kids are used to your strict rules. My boys weren't raised that way."

"Because I have rules and you don't, that doesn't mean I'm too strict." Barbara now has a bite in her tone.

By this point you probably can recognize their Right Fight. You also already know the answer: the two of them need to be more loving. The question that stands out now is, how?

Barbara's comments need to be shared in love, or as a free gift of her attention. Barbara is giving Wes plenty of her regard, but it is being expressed as negative/corrective and therefore is not being felt as love. What she has to say is valid, yet for Wes to "hear" it, the information must be shared without blame or criticism. Barbara's attention is not a gift, because it carries a demand to change. Actually, she has two expectations: the first is that Wes will see his problem parenting, and the second is that he will change it.

Before Barbara can speak "in love" she needs to focus on herself and take the focus off of Wes. Her regard is not free because she has yet to understand "what's wrong" as opposed to "who's wrong." She knows that Wes's actions are inappropriate, but she has not expressed what it is about that behavior that hurts or bothers her. Barbara is troubled by the issue but is not talking about her feelings—she is focusing only on his behavior. Since she does not know and understand all of the specifics of what is making her unhappy, these unidentified and unspoken emotions are preventing her attention from being given as a free gift.

Strong feelings carry an emotional charge that, in turn, draw and hold our attention. When our emotions are unconscious our regard remains unavailable. The next step for Barbara is to spend time freeing her attention by examining her feelings. Once she knows what is bothering her and why, then she will be able to share her feelings as a gift.

So Why Does That Bother You?

Taking a few moments out of the session, I focused her attention on herself. "Why does it bother you that Wes has two sets of rules?"

She answered, "Well, it's not fair."

I asked again. "I get that his bias is not just. But you are feeling personally attacked. What is it about his behavior that feels personal?"

Barbara responded, "Those are my kids. That's personal!"

Like most people, Barbara's feelings of upset were completely obvious to herself, and for me to ask for her to explain felt like a challenge. However, if she was going to focus on what was wrong and not who was wrong, she had to get in touch with the reasons underlying her feelings.

"Tell me more about why you think his behavior is about you. His actions clearly impact your life, but what do his deeds say about you and your kids."

After taking a moment to think, she replied. "It feels like his kids are more important than my kids."

Pushing for further details I asked, "How does that reflect on you?"

"When he gives them their way, he knows it irritates me, and it feels like he loves them more than he loves me."

Barbara had finally gotten to the issue she needed to discuss. The core of her upset was not that Wes was a bad parent. Rather, it was that Barbara interpreted his preferential treatment as meaning that he cared more about his children than about her. When she put this spin on his actions she was left feeling that he did not love her.

Barbara was trying to curb her feelings of being unloved by changing his behavior rather than by letting him know how she was interpreting his actions.

I asked her to face her husband. Then I asked her to repeat what she had just said, but this time directly to him. With tears forming in her eyes she shared. "I feel that you sometimes care more about pleasing your kids, than you do about pleasing me. I know you love your children. I don't want to stop that. However, I feel like when they are around you stop loving me and my boys."

Wes replied. "I'm sorry. I do love you. I guess I just go a little overboard when my three are around because I want to make up for all the time we are apart. But I don't mean to make you feel unloved."

~

The theme of all of their past conversations had been that Wes was a bad parent. Obviously, there was no way in which Wes was going to be supportive of Barbara's attack. As Barbara brought some attention to herself, she discovered her core feeling, and once she shifted her attention to her issue, Wes could get on board and be sympathetic toward her experience.

Communication works best when we first bring all our attention to ourselves.

By loving herself and focusing her attention on her feelings, Barbara created a shift in the conversation that allowed room for Wes to bring her attention, as well.

Barbara's issue was not that she did not love Wes. It was that she did not love herself. She was not focusing her attention on her feelings. Once she owned her upset, her husband could get on board.

To speak in love we have to love our neighbor/audience as we love ourselves. Originally, Barbara was doing neither. Communication was finally established when she gave attention to her issues and then freely shared what she discovered about herself with Wes.

How can you share blame as a free gift? It is not possible, because these critiques are not about us. All you have to give away is yourself. Your thoughts, needs, and emotions are what you have to offer. And that is always enough.

Exercise: "And . . .?

You need to love yourself before you can share your thoughts and feelings with your partner. Take a moment to bring some attention to yourself. Here is an exercise that will help you create an awareness of what feelings rest at the bottom of your upsets.

And ...?

Find an 8 ½ x 11 sheet of paper. On the top of the page, write out a conflict, a hurtful situation, or a grievance between yourself and your intimate partner. Keep it brief, one sentence. For example: "My partner never touches me unless he/she wants sex."

In the left-hand margin, below the stated problem, write the word "And?" This stands for, "And why does that bother me?"

Then write out what it is about your partner's behavior that upset you. After you write the answer down, write the question "And?" again. This time dig a little deeper and write down whatever comes up for you.

Repeat this process ten times. That's right, ten times! Each time you write out an answer, push harder for a deeper understanding of how it makes you feel, how it affects you personally.

Let us use the example above to illustrate the process.

"My partner never touches me unless he wants sex."

And? He does not just touch me he gropes me.

And? It's rude.

And? He does not show affection any other way.

And? It makes me not want to be touched.

And? It feels like sex is all he wants.

And? I am a sex object.

And? I feel like I do not matter to him.

And? I am not a person.

And? I feel like I am not special.

And? I feel like he does not love me.

Notice that as the responses come from deeper and deeper places within, a shift occurs. The focus moves from the partner to the self. There is more emphasis on personal feelings. In this example, the comments shifted from "you" to "I" statements. Look for the same change in perspective in your answers. Watch for a shift in focus as your responses move from comments about your partner's behavior to expressions of the feelings inside yourself.

The move toward self-understanding enables us to have a healthy conversation. Discovering what we are feeling is needed in order to know what to share/communicate. Once you have discovered the feelings that are at the core of your upset you will be able to go back to your partner and have a meaningful discussion.

If the exercise was difficult for you, you are not alone. In session, when I verbally go through the exercise with couples I often hear, "What do you want from me?" Irritated and defensive, most people have a hard time pulling out what they are feeling. To them it is obvious. Hence when I say back to them, "And why does that bother you?" the question feels offensive. Even when you read through the example above, it may seem that the question "And?" is discounting what was just said, as if what has been said is not good enough.

Pain produces a self-protective posture. When I am feeling hurt my attention naturally emphasizes the other person's behavior. This reaction is a normal part of our defense mechanisms. So it is a bit of a stretch to go against our instincts and open up when everything inside us is saying, "Shut down." Thinking about our upset causes us to bring up protective barriers to guard against further pain. Asking "and?" focuses attention deeper into the pain, so there will of course be some resistance, even when we are the ones pushing toward a deeper look inside our emotions.

Although it seems so difficult to relax our defensive posture long enough to look at our feelings, we already know the answer. When our spouse hurts us we feel unloved. A friend can safely joke about how I got lost last time the two of us went somewhere, but woe to my wife if she reminds me of the last time I did something wrong. I will feel offended. That is because we are all more sensitive to what our intimate partner says. If a friend hurts my feelings, I assume that he did not know better. When my partner hurts my feelings I assume that it was intentional. Thus, I tend to feel unloved.

The feeling of being unloved is often the true source of our reaction to our spouse's behavior. If she forgot to make the call you reminded her six times to make, it feels as to you as though she does not love you. When your spouse one more time is not interested in chatting when you are in a talkative mood, the feeling that comes up for you may be that she does not care. As difficult as it may be to get to the core of your feelings, you can jump-start the process by knowing that somehow the issue is going to be about feeling unloved. Go over your answers from your completed exercise and listen to yourself for these feelings of betrayal. See if you can identify the momentary mood of being unloved.

Emotional Pain Comes from the Brain

Not everyone is bothered by socks left on the floor. Some people do not care if their spouses watch TV. In fact, some couples enjoy curling up together. There are marriages where neither partner likes sex, while in other relationships couples have sex frequently. In some relationships, couples may spend a lot of time apart and it works well for them. The point is, our mood of hurt or betrayal is not directly linked to any particular behavior, but instead it is connected to the meaning we attach to our spouse's actions.

It is the meaning we place on

our partner's behavior

that creates our feelings.

Couples may mistakenly believe that emotions are a result of our partner's performance. There is no one behavior that would universally cause another person to feel unloved. Yelling or hitting to most people would be intolerable, yet there are families where screaming and even smacking is considered a normal part of the relationship. Even infidelity, in some cultures, is accepted. Our feelings may be stimulated by our partner, but our emotions are the result of our own interpretations and beliefs, not the consequence of their conduct.

Hurt, anger, frustration, and disappointment come from within ourselves. We need to remember that our feelings of "right" and "wrong" are like "left" and "right." They are self-references, expressions of how we see the world. The experience of being wronged is rooted in our perception of events. Unlike the directions of North and South, which can be verified by looking at a compass, there are no absolute truths that our partner can—or should—see and understand without our explanation.

Emotional pain is different from physical pain in that our feelings are *indirectly* prompted by events. If someone steps on your toe, receptors in your foot send signals to your brain and you experience pain. However, when you are feeling emotionally wounded, what happens is a little different. There is a stimulus. An event occurs. The brain then tries to figure out what happened and why it happened. Based on how we answer the question of "why?" we may or may not feel hurt. Emotional pain arises from an interpretation of a circumstance, and not from the situation itself.

Stepping on someone's toe does not hurt his or her feelings. However, if you believed that person had intentionally done it, then your feelings would be hurt.

Taking it one step (excuse the pun) further, imagine that it was not a stranger who walked on you, but that it was your intimate partner. The physical pain might not change, but the emotional wound increases as a function of the greater intimacy that already exists between you. The more you care, the more you hurt. Indeed, love increases vulnerability to pain. The person you live with knows what bothers you and what does not. If your partner upsets you there is no excuse, no ignorance to hide behind. For this reason, when your partner irritates you, the irritation may feel intentional, as if you have been wronged or are unloved.

Your crushed foot is factual. Your belief as to your partner's intentions is fiction. In your head you created a story about how your partner meant to do it. The beliefs you have formed cause your feelings to be hurt.

In order to discuss feelings with your partner, you both need to focus attention first on yourselves. Become aware of your interpretation of events. Then share your feelings as your own response, and not as a statement of blame directed at your partner. In this way, the door is open for a healthy dialogue.

~

Alfonso came in for his appointment complaining about his wife, Maria. He was upset that she was completely silent while they were having sex. He felt angry that Maria did not moan, squeak, or say a word when the two of them made love.

As strange as his complaint might sound, Alfonso had every right to his feelings. He was an auditory person and Maria's vocal sounds would have significantly enhanced his experience. When Maria was quiet he interpreted it to mean that she was not interested, was not being satisfied, and was not involved in their intimate occasion. As a result, Alfonso felt hurt and rejected.

Their problems did not stem from how Alfonso felt, but they most certainly were the result of how he dealt with his upset. Instead of talking about his own disappointment, Alfonso focused on his self-created perspective, that "Maria is a cold fish. She simply lies there. She is not excited about the relationship, so how can I be?"

Alfonso would do better by sharing *what* is wrong rather than pointing to *whom* he *thought* was wrong.

"I feel dissatisfied with our sex life." Alfonso can express anything as long as he talks about himself. "After making love I still feel disconnected. I don't feel any passion or excitement in what we do." His communication was better because he emphasized his feelings of dissatisfaction, and did not focus on Maria.

To express their feelings, couples have to understand why they feel the way they do. In order to accomplish this task, couples need to bring some attention to their individual selves and intelligently deal with their own emotions.

Earlier in this chapter we saw Barbara, irritated with Wes's double standard for his children and her. Yes, his actions were not fair, but what she interpreted (believed) when he displayed the preferential behavior was that his actions meant she occupied a lower priority in Wes's life. Barbara interpreted his behavior as a reflection that he loved his children more than he loved her.

To Barbara, it was a simple case of cause and effect. "He did this and I felt that." This perception is a setup for the blame game, because she took no responsibility in the situation. For her to avoid another battle over who is right and who is wrong, Barbara needed to focus her attention on herself. By being aware of her interpretation of events, she was able to focus the conversation on her feelings and avoid another *Right Fight*.

In the exercise, *"And . . . ?"* I used the example of someone never being touched except to prompt sex. In this case, the stimulus would be "only making contact for sex." The brain's response would be to work at figuring out why. In the moment we may tell ourselves, "It's because my partner thinks of me only as a sex object." And that thought makes us feel unloved.

The experience of not being loved must be expressed. This is truly *what is wrong.* Blaming or accusing our spouse of only wanting sex, or seeing us only as an object, is focusing on who is wrong. It is not taking responsibility for the fact that these are our observations. It is our interpretation of our spouse's behavior.

There is nothing right or wrong about our feelings. Irritation, hurt, frustration, and sadness are valid emotions. Everyone has a right to feel whatever he or she feels. What must change is that each of us must take responsibility for our feelings by owning them as a result of our thinking process and not as the consequence of our partner's behavior.

Exercise—Fill in the Gap

Here is another exercise that focuses your attention on yourself and reveals the thoughts that create our feelings.

Fill in the Gap

Take out a piece of paper. Divide it into three columns. In the left hand column write the word "behavior." In the second column place the words "my belief." The word "feelings" will head the last column.

Under the word "behavior" in the first column, write down a situation in your relationship that bothers you. Keep the description brief. Use a key word or a short sentence. Then skip to the last column, where you will write your "feeling" response. In this last column write either the word "hurt" or "upset."

Instead of struggling with finding the exact words that express your emotions, group them into feelings of pain or anger. The word "hurt" summarizes feelings of sorrow, rejection, abandonment, or that "unloved" feeling. The term "upset" will stand for all our angry feelings like pissed, frustrated, irritated, or annoyed. If you are experiencing both, write "hurt/upset."

In the middle column write the beliefs you tell yourself about their behavior. The center section will spell out the thoughts that create your hurt or upset. What is it that you believe was behind your partner's actions that would cause you to be feeling either sad or angry? It is in this middle column that the majority of your work will take place.

As an illustration, let us use Alfonso's anger with Maria. Being quiet during sex would go under the "behavior" column. Upset, or feelings of anger, would go under the "feelings" column. The work begins as he fills in the middle section. What belief does he have about his wife's silence that would make him upset? If she was mute or had laryngitis, he would not feel frustrated. So what is the meaning he puts behind her behavior that makes him so irritated?

Alfonso believes she is withholding attention. He interprets her silence as a refusal to give herself fully to him during their intimate occasions. "No attention" translates to "no love." Alfonso is angry because he believes Maria is not attracted to him.

Now complete the exercise for yourself. Discover what beliefs you have about your partner's behavior and then notice how these thoughts form the core of your emotions.

The Opposite of Blame Is Responsibility

What is going to stop the blame game? Each of us must take charge of our emotions. Blame shifts responsibility away from ourselves. Ending the *Right Fight* begins by looking at how each of us is accountable for our feelings. Then we can share our upset/hurt without conflict. The key is that we must bring attention to ourselves. We need to be liable for our emotions by understanding the consequence of our thoughts.

We want our partner's love and attention. We get it by first bringing our regard to our own feelings. Once we become answerable for why we feel the way we do, we can share our upset in such a way that our partner can hear us (using the techniques discussed in earlier chapters). Paradoxically, it is by first bringing attention to our issues, our feelings, and our upset that enables us to avoid the blame game.

Next comes another shift in attention. Even though you understand what you feel and why, it is still not time to talk with your partner about our pain. You need to prepare your spouse to hear you. This requires you now to shift your attention to your partner and to create a "connective place" in which your partner can truly attend to your feelings by hearing them, understanding them and responding appropriately to them.

Homework: Pay attention to why you feel the way you do. Regardless of what triggers you, for this week be aware of the spin your mind takes when viewing the different life events. Repeat the exercise "Fill In the Gap" with every emotionally charged event that occurs.

Chapter 16

Connecting

Come already happy, connected, and in love

The Naked Truth

Laticia came alone to therapy because her husband, George, would not have anything to do with counseling.

George's exact words were, "I don't need to go. I am not the psycho here."

According to Laticia it was George's defensive attitude that made it impossible for them to communicate. Laticia shared, "When I bring up any issue, he explodes in a rage."

After hearing a few examples of the volatile nature of their relationship, I let her know that there was something she could do. I told Laticia a story about a football coach who had a unique approach for disarming potentially explosive conversations. The coach would only discuss tough issues when a player was washing off in the shower room.

"Yeah Coach, you're right. I'll be more careful next time," was a typical response from the offending player. The coach had discovered that his players were much less defensive when they were undressed and vulnerable. Using the story as background, I suggested Laticia wait and talk to George when he was in the shower.

The following week she returned and told me what had happened. "It went beautifully," she beamed. "On the morning after our last session I went into the bathroom with George and began doing my make-up. Once he had climbed into the shower, I casually started to talk to him about a problem our oldest son was having at school. He didn't turn it around and start blaming me. He simply stood there and heard what I had to say."

It went so smoothly that later in the week Laticia decided to modify the homework. This time she exposed herself. She waited until George was in bed watching the news, then she undressed. "As I slowly put on my nightgown, I followed up with our son's problem. For the first time, George actually watched me as I talked. When I was done, he even made an observation. He pointed out that since it was a male teacher, maybe our son had an authority problem with men."

~

Like the coach in the story, Laticia discovered that being naked tends to create a sense of defenselessness. When there is no place to hide, people naturally move into a disposition of openness. Whether it is you or the other person who is unprotected, our vulnerabilities produce a state of connectedness, which then allows us to communicate.

Come Already Happy, Resolved, and "In Love"

By bringing attention to ourselves we have learned how to *calm* our emotional charge and also become *clear* about how our thoughts create feelings. But our attention is still not free. There is still a hidden agenda. We want to feel *close*.

To speak "in love," every word should be—like our attention—offered as a free gift, with no negative charge, no strings, no expectations. The motive underlying any dialogue should be to resolve the disagreement and thus to feel more connected. Oddly enough, these good intentions often prevent us from getting what we want. These agendas, well intended as they are, contaminate our conversations and create our Right Fights.

Sir Isaac Newton's third law of motion states, "For every action there is an equal and opposite reaction." Translated into relationship dynamics, this means that when we are in a protective or aggressive state, a similar state will be promoted in our partner. If we are disconnected when we begin a discussion, regardless of what is said, our spouse will match our mood and will disengage, as well. Likewise, if we approach our partner in a connected manner, our vulnerability will encourage our partner to be open and receptive.

Couples must feel *calm, clear* and, ultimately, *connected* before talking. Instead of coming to a conversation intending to vent or to confront a problem that is preventing them from being close, partners need to approach one another feeling close. The secret to effective communication is to come together already happy, already loving. Then whatever is discussed will only create a greater sense of closeness. It is *the connection*—not our communication skills—that will make our conversations effective.

Easier Said than Done

It is a nice sentiment to suggest we love those who hurt, anger, or frustrate us. There is one small problem. It goes against our instincts.

Negative internal and external dialogues set off the fight/flight response in everyone. This protective posture causes both partners either to withdraw or attack. Either reaction further divides the relationship.

To overcome this built-in, natural reaction we have to do the opposite. The suggestion to love is not an ideal to shoot for. Rather, it is how we counter these reactive patterns. Instead of closing down we need to open up. Rather than letting our attention collapse on our upset, attention/love needs to be brought to those who hurt us. Pushing ourselves to connect is how we extinguish our more primitive tendency to withdraw.

It is impossible to be relaxed and stressed at the same time. Our central nervous system (CNS) either places us in a panic mode or calms us down.

The same principle applies to our relationships. Our emotions serve one of two functions: they either serve to protect us, or they connect us. Like our situation with stress and relaxation, these states will not operate at the same time. We cannot be anxious if we are relaxed. Likewise, we cannot be protective if we are connecting. Being loving and vulnerable shifts us out of being defensive and guarded. This means our reactive patterns can be altered by changing our words as well as our actions.

To illustrate this point, allow me to use the example of a new couple in therapy. When couples come to my office for the first time, they often plop themselves down and begin reciting their list of grievances. I listen for a few moments to let the pair feel heard, but all they are focused on is who is right and who is wrong. Their negative emotional state never produces a positive connection.

As soon as possible, I interrupt and begin to change the tone of the conversation by asking the broad yet powerful question, "Do you love each other?" By redirecting the conversation toward what they love, I begin to sort out if we are doing couples counseling or divorce mediation. If the couple is willing to shift their attention and reconnect, the process can move forward. On the other hand, if either or both parties do not freely give their regard, I can accurately observe that there is a greater connection to the pain than to the partner. When one or both withhold or refuse love, it is highly likely that the marriage does not stand a chance. If a couple will not love each other until their issues are resolved, then their issues will never be rectified, and it is time for the two of them to move on.

When a couple answers the question in the affirmative (yes, we love each other), the course of the session almost always changes dramatically. As each of them begins to share about what he/she loves about the other, *physiological shifts begin to take place.* Smiles return, muscles relax, eyes begin to sparkle, partners begin to touch each other, and laughter fills the room.

Once the couple has come back to a connected place, I can begin probing as why they are in counseling. The answers I receive this time will have more to do with feelings than blame. Each will begin to talk about feeling lonely, afraid, hurt or frustrated. The petty details discussed in the beginning disappear.

Our Right Fights take us off topic, but by reconnecting the pair they begin to address the core issues that are disturbing them. Instead of talking about petty resentments such as how their partner does not take out the trash. The session focuses on the deeper issues of neglect behind the fact the trash was not taken out.

We Are What We Meditate Upon

As part of their protective patterns, couples continually remind each other of all the things their partner did or said—or did not do or did not say—that caused hurt and upset. Because attention is such a powerful bonding agent, the more the pair focuses on and discusses their grievances the stronger their mood of betrayal and unlove becomes. By focusing on the negatives the pair forgets, or fails to remember, what they also love about the other person. This in turn further strengthens their negative emotions.

Remember what you need to remember—to

stay connected and close.

Emotions, particularly reactive emotions, perpetuate themselves. It would be nice if when we became frustrated we could spend a few moments thinking about our frustration and the feelings would be processed and we would feel better. In truth, what occurs is that the more we dwell on the situation the more frustrated we become. Our emotions lead us to focus on our feelings, and our repetitive rumination about the circumstance further bolsters our upset. The more we think about our pain the further we move into that protective place.

This phenomenon becomes particularly problematic as we prepare to express our negative emotions with our spouse. Prior to any confrontation, most people spend time reflecting on what made them angry, hurt or sad. The more they think of what went wrong the more they stay in a protective state.

To come to a conversation connected a couple needs to also remember what they need to remember to stay in love. *You are what you meditate upon.* Another way of saying the same thing is, "What you focus on, you will create." Love binds us, so our loving attention strengthens that to which it is given.

We can see this very clearly in our parenting. Our attention to our children, even negative attention, reinforces behavior. If we focus exclusively on our child's poor conduct, the child is more likely to act out with more poor conduct. On the other hand, when we praise the activities we want, our kids are more likely to perform them. What we entertain in our brains will influence not only how we think, feel, and act, but also the actions of others with whom we come into contact.

In order to overcome a protective posture in ourselves, it is important to remember what we need to remember to stay in love. We may be filled with all kinds of feelings of hurt, sorrow and disappointment concerning our significant relationship, but if we allow our minds to meditate solely on the events associated with these negative feelings we will drop into a guarded position. To counteract this tendency we need to also remember the happy, romantic, loving, connecting events and the personal characteristics that brought us into intimate connection in the first place.

Recall and Re-connect

Most families are so busy these days that their discussions are often limited to talk about the tasks of the day or plans for tomorrow. Life is so hectic that a couple's conversations become limited to comments about all the unpleasant details of life, the things that went wrong, thus creating negative associations between partners. The quickest and most effective way to bring a couple together is to dialogue about pleasant experiences. In counseling, instead of reinventing the wheel, I find that the easiest way to get a couple to get back to a connecting space is to ask them to recall times when they were feeling closer.

One of memory's qualities is that it includes both factual information and emotional recall. Try this for yourself. Think about your first car, your first kiss, a beloved pet, or a moment of great personal achievement or recognition. Can you also remember the feelings that accompanied these memories? Probably, and the longer and harder you think about those good times, the more strongly you will feel the emotions that surround the factual memory. That is why it is so enjoyable to sit around with old friends and rehash times gone by—because it brings back the "good-old" feelings, as well. We put pictures into our photo albums because it helps us to remember all the good times, but when we look at the pictures we feel the feelings that were pleasantly present at the moment the photo was taken.

Every year Lucy's family got together for a reunion. Usually, the first couple of evenings proved boring for all the kids and in-laws as her and her brothers retold the same old stories. It was their way of reconnecting after being apart for so long. There were no real opportunities to renew their relationships during the year, so talking about the past recaptured their old feelings for each other and helped reestablish their friendships.

Couples certainly are around each other much more frequently than once a year, but still there often seems to be little time to connect, and rarely do we recount with each other about the good times we have had.

Before starting a conversation about some hurtful or difficult topic, spend just as much time first recounting some of the good times together. As a part of your daily discussions with each other, spend time talking about the pleasant times you have spent together. Pulling memories from the recent past is slightly more effective, because the details are fresher, and so are the associated feelings.

Let me suggest that you experiment by discussing your last vacation away from home. Once apart from life's normal distractions, couples typically give each other attention. As a result, family trips and time spent traveling together usually produce fondly remembered images and experiences. By remembering these events a couple will recapture feelings of closeness, and prepare themselves to dialogue about more difficult issues.

Remember, if your partner is a visual lover, make lots of eye contact as you describe images from your well-loved scene. Talk about the beauty of the fall trees, the brilliant red, yellow and orange leaves you both loved on your honeymoon trip back east. Create a mental picture of the details surrounding the scene or event that you want to recapture.

Use descriptive language that best fits your partner's style to flesh out the details and rekindle the feelings. "Remember the wonderful time we had at the ball game last year? It was so nice to hold hands and share the energy and excitement of the game." The kinesthetic person will recall the physical attributes of the soft sand and warm waters of your vacation to Hawaii.

Auditory people, on the other hand, need the sounds and activities around them kept to a minimum in order to be able to focus their attention on what is being said. For an auditory partner, use the language and phrases that he or she most closely identifies with, and be very aware of sounds and the vocal tones you use in conversation. "What I loved most about our date last Saturday was how nice it was to sit and talk without any distractions."

The key here—regardless of the learning style of your partner—is *not to make your conversation into a demand*. Talk about all the details that help you reawaken the feelings of closeness, but do not require that your partner do the same. The responsibility for your own emotional state is yours, and the objective in connecting is to turn your mood around. If your spouse comes about, as well, then that is all the better, but it is not the point. Talking about positive events will trigger memories and feelings for your spouse, of course, but if your stories come with a subtle requirement to participate, what you share will be resisted.

Try this activity as a refresher. Take the gratitude list you created when you calmed yourself down (in Chapter 14) and spend a minute or two sharing it with your spouse. Writing out a daily gratitude list will keep your heart soft. Casually sharing it every day with your partner will help to keep the bond between the two of you close.

Here again, draw out the details by using descriptive praise. After sharing what a good parent you think your spouse has become, for example, reflect on a recent situation that best illustrates why you think that he or she does well with the kids. "I was really impressed with how you handled Jimmy's tantrum in the store. I would have broken down and given him the stupid toy."

When there have been years of neglect and tension between two people, there are not many easily recallable "good times" to draw upon. In this situation, couples need to dig deeply and pull up events that occurred years ago. In session, I sometimes shift a couple into a positive space by asking them about their dating years.

Some of the typical answers I get are: "We loved sitting on the roof of his apartment and watching the sunset," or "Our favorite thing to do was to jump in the car and simply drive. We would talk and talk and end up wherever." Recall the best years of your relationship and talk about them prior to talking about any negative feelings of hurt or upset.

This is not a technique to manipulate the conversation by saying something nice prior to criticizing the other. True re-connection takes far more energy, time, and attention—and is therefore far more effective—than what we so typically see. One partner praising the other for making breakfast and then leveling a hostile criticism for some real or imagined affront, like having failed to phone is not it. To say a kind word does not divert a disagreement. When you say something nice and then take it back (by leaping into a critical mode), your partner quickly learns to not trust your praise, because at any moment you may do an emotional "about face" and call him or her a jerk

It may be that you do not have the time to spend talking about all the good times prior to sharing your upset. What needs to be remembered is that we are what we focus upon. Therefore, instead of thinking all day about how you were slighted, write the event down, or rehearse it once in your mind, and then spend time dwelling on the good. Remember whatever you need to remember that will keep your heart soft.

Watch for the physical signs that indicate your physiology is changing. Before bringing up anything disturbing, be sure you have shifted into a calm and connected place. Your emotional state has some elasticity to it, so take your time and wait until you see indicators that the connection is occurring—relaxed shoulders, stomach, and back, and/or a softness to your voice.

Newton's first law of motion says that an object in motion tends to stay in motion, and an object at rest tends to stay at rest. The same is true for your emotions. Once your relationship has moved into a disconnected place, one or both of you will remain distant until or unless a greater energy of force is applied to bring you back together. When one or both of you feels extremely hurt, it will take at least as much positive energy to pull you out of the slump as the negative energy it took to put you there in the first place. Be patient. Take all the time needed, and bring to the situation all the attention required to re-establish a real connection.

It may take a minute, a day, or a week, but what we are suggesting is that before you even think about sharing your pain, make sure you and your partner have, at least for the moment, become close and connected. Check within yourself for the return of those old feelings and watch for the signs within your partner that he/she is feeling affectionate. Only then should you risk moving into your pain at any level.

Act "as if"

The pattern that causes couples to distance from one another can also be interrupted simply through changing behavior. We can reverse the tendency to withdraw by acting "as if" we are in love.

Most of us have the sequence of events reversed. We think that changes in our behavior result from how we feel. More accurately, behaviors influence feelings. And since that is so, you can prompt new feelings by shifting your behavior.

You can experience this process at a time when you are "down," maybe even truly depressed. Generally, when you become melancholy you tend to feel hopeless and helpless. The result: you isolate. However, if you will do the opposite—get out of bed, get dressed up in something nice, go out and be around people, put a smile on your face (no matter how difficult this may seem—or even be—when you actually do it) and walk tall, invariably you will feel better.

Translated into relationship terms, know that by acting "as if" you are in love with your partner you will start to feel more loving. Therefore, before you begin a discussion with your spouse, arrange the situation so you can sit together, make eye contact, touch . . . the feelings will follow.

The moral: *it is easier to act our way to new feelings than to feel our way into new actions.*

You cannot be distant and disconnected when you are acting close and caring. Try having a discussion about a difficult issue while you are resting your head in the other person's lap. It will be almost impossible to fight. In the same way you can try giving your partner a warm hug and a passionate kiss. This will place you in the space where all is well.

The first thing I do when a couple in counseling wants to talk about an issue is to have them look at one another. When two people begin to squabble they almost immediately break eye contact. By asking them to look deeply into one another's gaze, I force each one of them to see the partner as a person, not solely as an object of frustration. Gazing into one another's eyes, helps immeasurably to induce a feeling of calm, quieting the emotional storm that brought the couple to my office in the first place.

When next you become angry with your spouse, focus your attention not on your anger but on the other person. Can you notice something good that you have not seen before, or can you find something pleasant about that person, something you really enjoy or appreciate? Maybe she has lost weight or changed her hairstyle slightly. Look for a cute mole or a freckle you have not noticed before. Maybe he is wearing a new shirt, an attractive sweater or has just had a badly needed haircut. As you search for something new that you like, two things will probably happen quite naturally: first, you will stop thinking so hard about what it was that was making you angry and, second, your shift in attention will soften your heart towards your partner.

To fix your gaze on the other person, as suggested earlier, is just one way of bringing you and your partner together. A light, considerate touch, on the upper arm, knee or hand will also help to ground you both. The physical contact will most likely place both of you in a receptive space.

Sit in your partner's lap before starting.

Touching, works for all types of people. Obviously, for kinesthetic people touch means a lot, but even for less "physical" folk, contact often produces a "grounding" feeling for emotions. In fact, a general rule I use is that before beginning a difficult discussion couples need to make some sort of physical contact, touching his arm, or leaning up against her. These simple gestures neutralize significant amounts of negative emotion.

～

Family functions are stressful, often creating added tension in a relationship, and that was exactly what was happening with Kevin and Sarah. They were on their way to her family's house for Thanksgiving dinner. Things were not going well. An argument seemed to be brewing about how the day would go.

In their counseling session a week before, they had been given the assignment of "touching" whenever either sensed a conflict. Remembering what was asked of them, Sarah broke off their rather tense discussion, saying, "Wait, let's hold pinkies first." The moment the two of them started to lock their little fingers together both of them "forgot" what it was they were fighting about. The physical contact dissolved the conflict because it had put them both in a place of connectedness.

～

The effectiveness of physical contact will correspond directly with the amount of attention you bring. If you mindlessly engage in the activities that have been suggested, then the results will be minimal. Conversely, if you give your complete regard to touching your spouse as you talk, then an emotional "bond" will occur.

I saw an instance of this recently in my office. I had suggested that Mike should "caress" his spouse's arm. Without making any eye contact at all, Mike reached over toward his wife, began rubbing a spot on her arm, and continued rubbing, in a circular pattern, over and over in the same spot. As you might think, his action did nothing for his wife, and soon she pulled away as if he had only irritated the spot on her arm. In fact, she began rubbing it herself as if to remove the feeling left behind when she rejected his gesture. Clearly, Mike had given essentially no attention to the contact. It was a mechanical gesture. There was no connection. He complied with the request, but his attention was on himself and, predictably, his touch had no positive effect.

Emotional Fuse

Physical contact also acts as an emotional "fuse." In an electrical circuit, a fuse prevents the electrical wires from becoming over-charged, which would cause them to overheat and start a fire.

Eye contact and handholding occur when the level of emotional charge between two people is low. When couples start off bringing attention to the other person and then withdraw, it is probable that one or both of them has become emotionally overloaded. When one or both parties in a conversation become too upset to maintain a gentle gaze or touch, then it is probably time to end the conversation, as well.

~

As Louis and Jan sat down on my office couch, Jan cuddled up against her husband as if he was a big pillow. He wrapped his arm around her waist. Immediately, I could see the stage was set for Louis to share.

Louis and Jan had not make love in years, but I saw that the two had reconnected enough so that he felt safe to reveal the resentments that were holding him back. But as Louis talked, I could see that Jan was beginning to personalize his pain. She moved out of the "cuddle" position and sat more upright on the couch. As soon as she moved away from Louis and shifted to the other side of the couch, Louis stopped the discussion and checked in with Jan. "What's the matter? Are you alright?"

The fuse had been broken and the physical connection had been lost. For either of them to continue with the conversation clearly would have produced greater tension.

~

Large issues carry an intense emotional charge for both parties. There is no way that Louis and Jan could discuss such deep pain and not become upset. It could easily take several weeks or months for these two to hash out all the details behind their lack of sexual intimacy. But by being aware of when to proceed and when to stop, both of them had learned how to prevent a further deepening of their wounds.

Homework: Connect before you have any discussion. Begin to get into the habit of making a physical connection prior to having any kind of dialogue. Each time you sit down to talk about the kids, your day, and the weather, make sure the two of you are making some kind of physical contact.

Chapter 17

Confessing

Talking about our pain

The Hostile Hostess

As a young man, I worked as a waiter to help pay my way through college. At one particular restaurant I encountered a hostess whom I just *knew* hated me. The two of us never had a fight. We did not even talk. But every time I looked at her looking at me, I felt daggers in her gaze. It baffled me for a while, but it turned out that our religious differences were the source of her irritation. I was a Christian and she was a Muslim.

One night after closing time, when the staff was sitting down for dinner, I dropped my head to pray. At that moment the "hostile hostess" removed the lid from the saltshaker and poured the entire contents on my meal. I looked up just as she completed her mission. All kinds of choice words passed through my brain, but I said nothing . . . to her or to anyone else. I simply got up, took my plate to the kitchen, and asked the cook to redo my meal.

For the next hour I was mad—no, I was furious. Finally, I realized that being angry was not hurting her. In fact, it was just what she wanted by way of emotional response from me. In that moment, I had a choice to make. I could hold on to my anger or not. I decided to have a little talk with the "enemy."

"I want to say I'm sorry. For the last hour I've been walking around here holding on to all kinds of bitterness over what you did at dinner. I don't like carrying around those kinds of feelings. I'm not interested in being angry with you. So, I wanted to say that I'm sorry for holding resentments toward you, and I am really sorry for whatever I might have done or said that made you want to do that in the first place."

With that, I walked away, not caring what she did. I harbored no futile hope that perhaps now she would like me. My response to the whole episode had nothing at all to do with wanting her to own her behavior. *I simply wanted to rid myself of those negative feelings.*

Did I need to apologize to her? Yes and no. Yes, because it helped me feel better to take responsibility for my anger. But it was not owed to her as if I was the one who poured salt on her meal. The apology was not for her. It was for myself.

The hostess was responsible for her own actions. My emphasis was on myself. By confessing my reaction I was able to clear off my side of the street and walk away free of all my negative emotions. At one level it was a purely selfish gesture in that I knew that by owning and sharing my emotions I would feel better. So that is what I did, and that is exactly what happened.

By the end of the conversation I felt open and free. The tension I had been feeling had finally shattered. The anger had disappeared. She could have talked with me and I would have been completely comfortable, open to anything. She never did, and that was fine too, because I had no further expectations.

The story of the hostile hostess is an example of self-love through good communication. As a tool to promote change in our spouse, to point out his/her mistakes, our conversations fail. However, when our discussions are used to express ourselves and release our upset our dialogues are the most effective means we have. People can share their thoughts, feelings and needs in even the most hostile of environments and still walk away happy.

Confession

Before we explore the secrets behind a healthy verbal interaction, we need to find a new term that will differentiate our suggested solution from the old and unhealthy patterns we are all so used to. "Communication" is too broad a word to be useful. It does not distinguish between appropriate and inappropriate interactions. Thus far, we have used adjectives like "real" or "true" to denote a new style of expression. But the term "true communication" still does not provide enough distinction regarding what should or should not be said.

The word *"confession"* more accurately describes what needs to occur when two people talk. A confession involves

1) sharing information about our self, while

2) taking complete responsibility for our beliefs, emotions, and actions.

Confessing our feelings to someone is an act of vulnerability. To confess to feeling hurt means that we are exposing our wounds.

We cannot confess to the fact that someone else committed a crime. In the same way, we cannot confess to how *our partner* hurt us, made a mistake, fell short, or did something wrong. A confession is about *our* choices. It is a vehicle for taking ownership of our feelings, thoughts, and actions.

The *other* person may have triggered your emotions, but the message is clear that being angry is how *you* chose to respond. Responsibility for our own actions is always directed back to ourselves.

Since a "confession" focuses on the self rather than on the other, all we need from a partner is an acknowledgment that what we have said has been accurately heard. A confession does not require a response. There is no need for the other person to fix things or make the situation all right.

Notice how the technique of describing our conversations as "confessions" includes both elements conveyed in proper communication. We have already learned that an effective intimate conversation focuses on the self and is, at its root, a sharing of our experiences and an expectation only to be heard. A confession has a focus on the self rather than the other, and a goal of simply being listened to without emotional "interference."

It's All about Me

Talking is the primary means in which couples take care of their needs and thus love themselves. Opening up to a significant other focuses attention on feelings and desires. Telling your partner about your pain brings attention to your problems and provides a way for releasing the negative emotions that pain produces. Consequently, you feel better, and your relationship improves when you communicate properly.

Confessions are purely selfish.

As we have already pointed out, to get attention we have to give ourselves attention. Our confessions are not only a form of self-love—a way to draw notice to our feelings, thoughts, and needs—but true communication only occurs when we direct our regard toward ourselves. To be listened to by our mate we have to focus on ourselves. It is a counterintuitive situation, but the more self-focused our dialogue, the more likely we will be heard.

The hostess story that begins this chapter is an example of how confessing my own experience gave me the attention I needed. If my discourse had in anyway emphasized her behavior or implied that I was not responsible for my own feelings and reactions, I would never have gotten what I needed. By talking exclusively about myself I was able to express my upset and thus release my anger. *Making that conversation about me gave me what I wanted.*

~

Sarah is angry with Kyle for forgetting their anniversary. Her anger is what it is. By its existence alone, it does not prevent the two from remaining close, as long as Sarah confesses her feelings. If Sarah says, "I am angry because you forgot," then her emphasis makes him responsible for her upset. To be "confessed" she must take full responsibility for her emotions.

"Kyle, I need to let you know that when you did not give me a card, or even say 'Happy Anniversary,' I felt hurt and angry. I do a lot for our relationship throughout the year, and I had an expectation that you would give a little on our anniversary. Because you did not meet my expectations I got mad. Do whatever you want with this information, but I needed to let you know, because I have been pulling away ever since."

~

Sarah's confession is an example of expressing what is wrong as opposed to who is wrong. The problem is not that Kyle makes her angry. The issue is that she had expectations that he did not fulfill, and that caused her to feel hurt and in turn, angry. Without either shaming or blaming Kyle, Sarah simply expresses the facts as they occurred. Sarah does not give in to her anger and attack him. She instead lets Kyle know exactly what she is feeling. Her confession does not negate her needs. Rather, it clarifies their existence.

Couples are often caught between a rock and a hard place. Either they express their anger and push each other away, or they hold their anger inside and end up pulling back. It does not matter if the stone hits the pitcher or the pitcher hits the stone, it is always bad news for the pitcher. Similarly, regardless of whether we rebuff or retreat, the relationship suffers.

Couples can and should express their upsets by remaining confessed. True confessions enable couples to share their upsets and, in doing so, to become even more intimate.

~

"Stop interrogating me."

Jack was frustrated at his wife's questions. His comment emphasized his spouse's behavior. A more effective confession would have been, "When you ask me questions over and over about where I have been, it makes me feel like you don't trust me, like I am a bad kid who needs constant supervision. I don't know if that is what you mean to do, but I find myself wanting to tell you even less." That sort of comment would have stressed Jack's experience over his wife's actions.

~

Couples are driven to conversation because it is an essential way to demonstrate love, both for themselves and for each other. Talking about emotions and desires makes the partners aware of who they are and what they want, and in doing so they also experience the added benefit of momentarily capturing their regard for each other.

A Monologue-- Not a Dialogue

The most unusual characteristic of our confessions is that they are, in essence, more monologue than dialogue. Sharing one's feelings as an authentic confession, does not imply or display any expectations. Therefore, there is no need for the listener either to agree or disagree. Yes, we need to feel as though the other person is listening, but beyond that the expectations have to end. There need be no discussion, no dialogue between the two parties.

It should be pointed out, as well, that exchanging ideas rarely works out. If our partner shares his/her thoughts directly on the heels of what we have said, *we do not feel heard*. The only way we will be happy with our spouse's remarks is if they correspond perfectly with ours. Otherwise, the conversation will shift to a Right Fight, with each party focusing on why his/her ideas are correct, and/or why his/her partner is wrong.

~

Kathleen came to counseling not really interested in learning how to save her marriage. Instead, she wanted to know how a divorce would affect her children. She was done. All she wanted was to get out with as little damage to her children as possible.

When I asked her what was so bad about her marriage she replied, "I am the kind of person who needs to talk, and when I do, all he does is sit there, saying nothing."

Kathleen was interpreting her husband's quietness as disinterest and was therefore no longer interested in continuing the relationship.

~

She was making two mistakes. First, she was not taking personal responsibility for her own mood of unlove.

Over time, Kathleen had become increasingly unhappy with her life. As this process was unfolding and her unhappiness was descending toward depression, she began to search for the cause of her melancholy. Early on, she noticed that conversations with her husband were failing to make her feel better. She also observed that their discussions were always one-sided, with her talking and him listening without responding. It was quite natural, then, that Kathleen soon came to believe that her sharing did not—and perhaps could not—satisfy her needs because her husband did not participate with the same intensity. The moment she interpreted his quietness as the cause of her feeling unloved, the relationship began to slide downhill at a rapid pace.

Her husband had always been restrained. In fact, his quiet disposition had been one of the qualities that first attracted her. In the intervening years, he did not change—she did.

To feel unloved

is part of the human experience;

it is not a fault of either

your spouse or your marriage.

We all feel unloved from time to time. It is part of the human experience. But instead of seeing her feelings for what they were—expressing her opinion, not necessarily the facts of the matter—Kathleen blamed her husband. At that point her beliefs became a self-fulfilling prophecy through which the more Kathleen came to believe that her husband no longer loved her, the less love flowed between them. The stronger her conviction became that his silence was an indication of his withdrawal, the more quiet and withdrawn he seemed to become.

Her second error came in not understanding what true communication looks like. When we confess our feelings there is no need for discussion. "This is how I feel."

What more could—or should—possibly be said in response than "I hear you" or "I understand" or "I get it." Dialogue in this situation boils down to a short feedback message that assures the speaker that the listener really "hears" what is being confessed.

Confessing her unhappiness would have prevented this enormous misunderstanding between Kathleen and the man who loves her. She needed to cuddle up in her husband's arms and let him know that she was feeling unloved. "Sweetheart, I've felt distant and disconnected the last few days, and as a result I've been rather sad. I don't need you to say or do anything, these feelings are mine, but I do appreciate you holding me as I talk."

How does that help? How can a one-sided conversation make a person feel connected? Unfortunately, Kathleen's mistakes are representative of the misconceptions that many, many couples adopt and nurture over time. We all feel unhappy at times. But by staying current with our feelings and sharing them as "confessions of selfhood," couples can remain close.

The healing comes through sharing our feelings. Healthy conversations function similarly to how good friendships or even therapy operates. Even though the events may be in the past, and therefore are unalterable, we feel better after confessing them to another human being. We do not need our friends to do something to take away our hurt, sorrow, and anger. Emotions are energy in motion. Hence, by talking about our feelings we can release them and bring healing to our lives.

The fundamental problem that Kathleen was having with her "communication" was that she was not using it as a way to *give* herself attention but as a method for trying to *get* attention.

Smoking Mad

Irene and Andrew found each other after previously bad marriages. The two met while she was finishing her medical training at a hospital where Andrew was a staff physician. Their plan, once Irene had finished her residency, was to marry and start their own family medical practice.

However, a snag cropped up. Andrew took up cigarette smoking. Time after time he promised to quit, but his addiction was too strong.

Because the smoking issue was precipitating frequent, huge blowouts, Irene decided to try a style of communicating she learned in counseling with her first husband. The technique was called, "when you . . . I feel."

"When you go off to smoke," Irene would say, "I feel lied to. I feel I am just not important to you. When you duck outside between surgeries, I think you see me as stupid because you don't think I can smell it on you."

Andrew retorted, "You're not stupid, you're a control freak. Who made you the smoking police? This is my life! If you don't like it, you can leave." Despite Irene's best efforts, the conversation quickly erupted into a huge screaming match.

~

Irene used "I" messages and threw in a few "I feel" statements. Her effort still failed because what she was expressing was not a true confession. She was neither talking authentically about herself nor expressing her true feelings.

Her "confession" implied that he was lying to her and did not value her opinions. Finally, she sent him a message that she believed that he considers her to be stupid. These are not confessions. They are, at best, attempts to "correct" his behavior by pointing it out as negative.

What was she really feeling? Under scrutiny, we can see that the term "lied to" is not a feeling. Rather, it is a statement about the other person's behavior. In fact, no one could tell from the words themselves just what feeling Irene was experiencing.

In her anger she conveyed the message that she was upset, but the "when you … I feel" method put at least equal emphasis on his actions while not completely describing her feelings. Irene's attention was not being given freely to Andrew or to herself. Therefore, she was not communicating in love.

Her problem was that she had done none of the four steps involved in communicating. Irene wrongly used her discussions to calm herself. She did not spend any time identifying what she was feeling, nor had she made an attempt to connect with Andrew prior to their conversation.

At the end of our visit I gave Irene some "homework." I asked her to begin applying the "4 'C's." When Irene got home she composed herself by taking a long walk. After returning to the house, she spent time clarifying her issues by doing the "And . . .?" exercise. Sitting down with a pad of paper, Irene started the exercise by writing out a short statement of what was bothering her. "Andrew's smoking." On the next line she wrote, "And?" which was short for, "and why does that bother me?"

What came up first for Irene was that both of them were doctors. "He knows the health risks."

On the next line she dug a little deeper. " . . . And . . . why does it bother me that he knows the health risks?" Her answer came through almost immediately. "That bothers me because he does not care about living a long life together."

When she asked herself the question "And?" it became clear that Irene intuitively "got" that Andrew was not paying attention to how his smoking might affect their future together.

After asking herself, "Why does it bother me that he does not think about the future?" her insight became even clearer. "I care more about this relationship than he does."

With one final probe of her feelings, Irene came to the conclusion, "I love him, but I am not loved in return."

At that point, Irene began to recognize that she had spent her life trying to win the approval of the men in her life, and never feeling good enough.

After spending time soul-searching, Irene felt emotionally spent, but she was calmer and clearer. However, she was still disconnected.

Irene decided to bond through service. Going to the market she picked out the freshest ingredients, returned home, and prepared her husband's favorite meal. It took her a little over an hour, but she spent the entire time thinking about all the things she admired about him. By the time the meal was cooked and ready to serve, her heart was open and she was prepared to confess her upset. Here is her confession as she recalls it.

"Honey, I want to let you know why your smoking bothers me. When I discover you've had a cigarette, I tell myself you smoked because I am not that important to you. I have convinced myself that you don't care and that smoking is your way of demonstrating that.

"Then when you lie about smoking, it makes my insecurities even worse. I start thinking, 'What else is he lying to me about?' At that point, I look back on all the good times we've had and think that maybe those were all lies, too. I tell myself, 'He was just acting as though wanted to be with me.'

"I never admitted this to you—or even to myself—because it sounds so stupid. And I've been afraid I'd find out it's true. So there it is. That's why I flip out when you light up."

Irene's second attempt at sharing her feelings was much more of a true confession because she shared herself.

She did not need Andrew to agree to stop smoking or even to try. All she was asking was that he listen to her true feelings. Irene did not require anything of him because she had already dealt with those feelings and was using her emotions as a way to make herself vulnerable, thus connected.

Spending time identifying her upset had also relieved her pain significantly and had helped her come closer to a place of closure. All that was left was for her to communicate. Irene had really loved herself by focusing attention on her own feelings, and in doing so she was able to take responsibility for the emotions those feelings had produced.

Andrew responded with genuine concern in his voice. "I had no idea! The reason I always try to hide my smoking is that I'm embarrassed by it. Each time I give into the desire to smoke, I feel like a failure. I feel weak. I hate myself, so I assume you'll hate me, too."

For every action there is an opposite and equal reaction. Irene's confession had prompted a sincere acknowledgment from Andrew. What she needed from Andrew, openness and honesty, she had to first provide. When she brought him her heart he reciprocated by sharing his as well.

Getting What We Want

Being confessed is essential in expressing our feelings, but it is also a means for asking for what we want. To convey our needs, the same rules apply. Our confession must be a free gift of our attention. To express our desires "in love" we must, 1) focus on ourselves, and 2) take responsibility for our needs.

~

Katherine finds that even a quick trip to the market can be harrowing when her husband, Lee, is driving the car. "Lee doesn't know how to be relaxed behind the wheel. He tailgates, speeds, and swears at everyone around us. My nerves become shot anytime he drives."

Although the problem is legitimate, it is not really Lee's issue, it is Katherine's. Katherine is indicating that her partner has a problem with driving when, in truth, he does not, she does. In this case, Lee was not upset, not bothered at all by the way he drove, but Katherine approached the situation by casting him as the "bad guy." Hence, the only topic that surfaced was "Who was the good guy and who was the bad guy."

To talk about ourselves and take responsibility for our needs, we have to identify which issues belong to us and which are the property of our partner. The only way we can recognize that is to determine who believes there is a problem. Once we do that, confession becomes easy—and effective.

Being anxious when Lee drives is Katherine's problem. If she confesses this as her issue, she has a stronger chance at being heard and having her spouse respond. Would this response get the job done? Katherine confesses, "For years I have complained about your driving, and now I realize you're not the one with the problem, I am. You have never gotten in an accident or been ticketed. I guess the issue must be mine. So, when we travel together I would really appreciate it if I could drive. That way I can feel safe and relaxed."

~

When we ask for what we want in a relationship, it seems perfectly natural that we should place the emphasis on our desires rather than on our mate's shortcomings. But how we express that, the focus we put on our communication makes all the difference.

No one is going to respond well to this kind of request: "It would be nice if once in a while you would do the dishes."

A better approach would be to take responsibility for your needs. "I don't like to leave dishes in the sink, but I don't have time to get to them. It would be a great help if you could wash the dishes tonight." This request appropriately places ownership of your needs on yourself and is more likely to garner willing help as a response.

~

Jack was frustrated about his sex life with Nancy. "It feels like she is never interested."

Nancy enjoys having sex, but she does not like having it quite as often as he would like. Nancy is content with the frequency of their intimate occasions, so she is not motivated to make any changes. In this situation, in order to get his needs met Jack must recognize that the problem is his. Only by taking responsibility for his frustration will Jack be able to get what he wants.

"Nancy can we have a date (their euphemism for sex) tonight?"

"I have to finish with the kids' homework and then put them to bed." She is not saying no, but she is not saying yes.

Jack suggests, "How about if you take some time off, soak in a warm bath, and I'll take care of the kids for the rest of the evening".

Grinning delightedly, Nancy responds. "All right, that will work for me."

Debating whether Jack has the overactive sex drive or Nancy is unresponsive will not accomplish anything positive for either of them. If Jack wants to create more coupling time, then he must work from the knowledge that his level of desire is his issue, not Nancy's.

Necessity is the mother of invention. By owning his needs, Jack is motivated to make changes. When he pushes the problem on his partner, he places himself in a position of powerlessness. By taking responsibility for his desires, he takes control of his needs and increases his chances for getting what he wants.

If you are the one who is upset, then

—by definition— it is your problem.

Pain, frustration, hunger, sorrow, and unhappiness motivate people to take action. The one who is bothered by a situation is the one who is spurred to generate change. Therefore, passing off our needs onto someone who does not share our dissatisfaction will fail to produce the results we want.

There is a huge difference between getting others to love us and loving ourselves. We all intuitively understand that we cannot spend our lives solely loving others in the hope they will love us in return. We need to be loved without conditions and without restraints. Being confessed is not just another strategy to get our partner to do what we want. Confession—the honest, accurate statement of our true feelings and the emotions they engender—improves the chances of such love because it repairs misunderstanding, dispels confusion, and re-connects lovers as no other technique in relationship building.

The responsibility for bringing attention our way is ours. What goes wrong with our old strategy is that instead of bringing attention to our feelings, we direct our attention on our partner in an attempt to *get* his/her consideration. *To love ourselves we need to give ourselves attention.*

Homework: We need to learn to walk before we can run. In advance of tackling the big topics in your marriage, practice confessing your feelings about the small stuff. Three to four times this week, pick a situation that hurts or upsets you. Then step by step walk through the four "Cs." Focus your regard only on yourself. To do this you will need to be calm, clear on what your issues are, connected to your audience, and then finally confessed about your experience.

Epilogue: Marriage; It Just Ain't Natural

Addressing our resistance to love

"Don't Feel Loving . . ."

~

"He wouldn't do anything we talked about last week." Marta began our second counseling session by complaining about how Hank, her husband, had refused to do the homework I had assigned in our previous session.

Instead of addressing Hank's resistance directly and immediately, I spent a few minutes redirecting Marta, and after we had taken a quick review of the *"Four 'C's,"* Marta restated her tattling as an expression/confession of her fears.

"When you refused to do the homework it left me with doubts about the relationship. I felt you didn't care."

Once she was confessed, the conversation shifted to Hank, who responded, "I didn't do the assignment because it didn't feel natural."

Hank had been asked to give Marta a hug and a kiss twice everyday. He expressed his feeling that the behaviors were contrived and thus did not resonate as genuine. "I don't feel loving, so it is hard for me to act like I am."

~

You have to love Hank's honesty! The actions he was being asked to take did not *feel* loving (to him), so he could not *be* loving. Of course, this attitude, if he were to continue it, would eventually leave him without any relationship at all. His feelings brought the two of them together, but if he allows his emotions to set the pace his feelings will drive them apart.

Love Is Counterintuitive

Most creatures have specific behaviors imprinted on the brain to keep them alive. However, there are situations when following these responses will do more harm than good. Norway lemmings herd together as a part of their survival strategy. During their migration the herd of lemmings will at times reach the ocean and the leader will attempt to swim into the sea, as if it was crossing a river. The other lemmings will follow and result in hundreds drowning.

There are times when allowing our impulses to control our behaviors may be the wrong course of action because when we do so, the results are disastrous. Specifically, practicing love in what appears to be un-loving situations runs counter to the very human drive to distance ourselves from those who hurt us. Yet, if we let our protective reactions rule the day our relationships would never survive.

One of the best examples of how our human instincts can turn deadly can be seen when people are placed in a water environment. Even those who know how to swim can still drown if they begin to panic, because our basic protective impulses are adapted to life on land. When threatened, we keep our heads up, looking for danger. Our feet are beneath us, ready to run or attack. In the water, though, when we become erect we lose buoyancy. With our head up, we begin to sink, and all the energy we expend trying to keep our head above water is wasted. If we go against our impulses and allow ourselves to lie flat face down, and occasionally turn our head to take a breath, we can float effortlessly for hours.

For you non-swimmers, here is yet another example, one I am certain you can relate to if you ever learned to ride a bicycle. Before you mastered the art of balancing on a two-wheeled contraption, if the bike began to wobble, your first thought would be to slow down. But the slower you went, the less stable the bike became. You achieved mastery only when you learned to restore balance by *going against your impulses* and *increasing* your speed.

> *The problem is not psychological, it is physical: people recoil from pain.*

When we touch a flame, our immediate reaction is to pull away. The problem with this primitive recoil is that it is through our emotional heart that we feel all our feelings. When we withdraw from emotional pain, that same act has closed us off from feeling our love of our partner and the love our partner has for us.

If we do move away—and most of us do—we retreat into a protective stance, and we almost certainly begin evaluating negatively—and incorrectly—by focusing on who is wrong rather than on what is wrong. By retreating from pain, we lose touch with feelings of affection. Our conditioned response pulls us out of relationship, creating distance, not closeness, in our marriage.

In relationships, going with our most primitive instincts will direct us in exactly the opposite direction from where our best interests lie and where we most want to be. We need to realize that feelings are not facts. They are just emotional responses to what we perceive to be facts—in essence, they are only interpretations, and not necessarily accurate ones at that.

Feel Your Feelings, but Never Believe Them to Be True

An appropriate response to our negative emotions is to *feel the feelings, but never believe them to be true.* Do not act upon them as if they are reality itself. They are not. We need to be able to feel our feelings, because sometimes they protect us from harm or warn us against threats to our safety or happiness, yet we need also to recognize that emotions are subjective—they are about ourselves and our unhappiness, not a result of what another person may have done to us or said about us.

Our natural reaction to our negative emotions is to either ignore them or to act them out them through destructive behaviors. When we repress them we tend to reinforce the upset and increase the stress level we feel. And when we act out, it is often via an irrational, potentially damaging "explosion" through which we attempt to relieve the stress we are feeling. As you can easily see, both of these typical responses to pain tend to perpetuate the problem.

That we resist, tends to persist. Newton's second law of motion holds that the force we use to move or stop an object is equal to the mass of that object. Converting that premise into emotional terms, the more volatile our emotions, the more energy it will take to hold them back. To repress intense feelings of hurt will require an equivalent amount of psychic energy. The energy spent holding down these feelings will correspond with the amount of attention/love that will be drained or blocked. Hence, the more energy we use to hold back emotions, the less energy we will have available for loving ourselves or others.

Physical pain differs from emotional pain in one significant dimension. If my leg is broken, I can take enough painkillers to completely relieve my discomfort, but the painkillers will not interfere with the healing. The leg will get better anyway. Emotional pain, on the other hand, may be masked by many "painkillers"—alcohol, drugs, sex, money, food, and so on. But our emotional pain remains, and when the painkiller is discontinued the pain returns. Repression keeps our negative emotions alive while "stealing" the attention (psychic energy) we need to connect.

With emotional pain, *we must feel our feelings in order for the hurts to heal*. Yes, time may heal some emotional wounds, but most of our psychic pain will remain unless we approach it, feel it deeply, understand it and even open it up to others. As irrational as it may seem, we *must feel it in order to no longer feel it*. When feelings are repressed, healing does not occur.

The flip side of the problem is that when we do feel our feelings, we tend to give too much attention to our emotional charge and thus inadvertently reinforce our negative emotions. Attention/love connects us. Giving our regard to our spouse will bind us to him or her. In the same way, when we give our attention to our emotions, we will become more attached to our feelings. The more energy we give to our hurt, sorrow, and anger, the more we become hurt, sorrowful, and angry.

Emotions are different from physical sensations. When I "feel" cold I put on a coat and the sensation disappears. Likewise, when I "feel" hungry and then eat the hunger becomes satisfied. However, when it comes to emotions, the more we give them our regard the more the feelings are reinforced. If this were not true, fighters or football players would be very calm and peaceful people.

Our emotions are forever shifting and changing. Today I may feel "up" and happy. Tomorrow I may be feeling frustrated or withdrawn. This is because our emotions are easily influenced by outside factors. Being hungry, tired, or sick will alter our emotions, whereas an itch (a physical sensation) does not increase or diminish based on external influences.

When I go to the movies, I watch the images on the screen. The music, and the dialogue can have me feeling sad or afraid, angry, or in love. It is this fact, that emotions are so easily manipulated, that makes our feelings unreliable, as accurate tests of reality.

Although feelings are not facts, emotions can be made real. In a room full of strangers, an individual who focuses on the fear of not being accepted will attract fewer people than the person who believes that he or she is totally acceptable in that setting. There is a metaphysical concept that says, "We are what we meditate on." That translates, in practical terms to say, "The more attention I pay to my angry feelings, the more likely it is that I will get into a fight."

Our thoughts come and go and our emotions ebb and flow. None of us has control over what we think or feel. We can, though, determine how much our thoughts and emotions will influence our actions by choosing the amount of attention we bring to the process.

Recognizing Our Own Unhappiness

Emotional pain is a part of every relationship. In fact, it is those we love the most that can, and do hurt us the most. Instead of doing anything to rid ourselves of these feelings, we need to understand they are a natural byproduct in every relationship.

As we saw earlier, because we equate physical and emotional sensations, we believe that the same rules apply to both. When our body is damaged we experience physical pain. The pain receptor sites are letting us know there has been an injury and that part of our body requires special care. Naturally, that same logic is applied to our emotions, and when we feel hurt, sad, or upset, the belief is formed that something is wrong. At times this is true, while in other instances the emotional pain we feel is the result of how we see or interpret events.

Yes, you feel hurt, but as we have seen in Chapter 15, that does not necessarily mean that someone has hurt you. In fact, our feelings of sadness and/or unhappiness do not indicate that anything is wrong at all. More often than not, they are a normal part of our human state.

At the core of every person there is a sense or belief that we are not loved. Most of us bury these emotions but unconsciously act them out by picking someone who ultimately reinforces the experience of being unloved. The other course is to feel these emotions and then consciously to strengthen them by recoiling and withdrawing our love.

Psychologists believe that your pain comes from early childhood experiences in which your needs were not always met. Because no parent can satisfy all of a child's conscious and unconscious needs, each of us carry a certain amount of pain. It does not mean that we grew up in a bad home. Our feelings of sorrow and sadness are the result of unfulfilled desires. The more unhappy the home, the more unhappiness will be generated. However, because it is impossible to have a perfect family, we all carry some pain.

What happens when we get into a relationship and we open ourselves up to those we love is that we begin to experience the feelings of unlove or unhappiness that existed from past relationships. Even though our spouse is 90% better than anyone else we have been involved with, that 10% shortfall triggers, at times, all those old hurts to come back to the surface.

Psychology is not the only discipline to seek an explanation of the pain of our human condition. Religions have created their own interpretations. Eastern traditions hold that we carry pain from past life experiences. Even if everything about our lives was charmed, we still hold hurt from one of the other lives we have lived, so pain is an inevitable part of life.

The Western religious perspective states we were all born in sin. Therefore, we live in a condition of unlove. God is love, and ever since humans were kicked out of the Garden of Eden we have been separated from love itself. Disconnected from love, we all live in a state of unlove and unhappiness.

Whatever the religious, spiritual, or secular paradigm, we ascribe pain as inevitable. It is essential to recognize our mood of unlove as our own, created by our very existence—not as having been cast upon us by an outside person. As soon as we are able to see our pain as our own, we will be able to avoid becoming reactive to the pain and remain close to our significant other as we confess our feelings. There is no doubt that our intimates do or say things that trigger our negative feelings, but be wise and understand the pain is only in part due to our partner.

Assume Love

Instead of doing anything to escape your feelings of unlove, concentrate on generating feelings of love. What it takes is the ability and willingness to always assume love—consciously.

Whenever you recognize feelings of unlove within yourself, refocus on love. Feel your upset, *confess* it to your significant other (or to whomever the feeling relates), but always assume (believe) that there is love between you.

253

Yes, your partner may have said something that was hurtful to you. But remember, no one can hurt our feelings. We feel pain because of our own interpretations, or as the result of our childhood, or through karma. You do have the right to feel your upset. You also have the obligation to write about it, think about it (constructively), even to share it with an uninvolved friend, but then continue to bring your attention back to the love of those around you—your love for them and their (assumed) love for you.

Understand that we all go through periods of temporary insanity. Do not believe that madness to be true, otherwise you both will go crazy.

Set boundaries with one another in reasonable ways, and express your needs in appropriate terms. Confess your feelings honestly and subjectively (it is about me, not about you). But do it all through the free gift of your attention. Do not let your attention become so collapsed in your upset, that you forget to love or do not remember the love of those around you.

At the end of the day, if the two of you cannot continue to be together, then move on, but always assume (believe) that you love that person and that person loves you. If you divorce, do it in love.

At one point in my relationship with Lynda I remember confessing to her the classic line, "I love you, but I am not 'in love' with you." To this day, her response brings tears to my eyes. She replied, "I know you love me. You may not feel it right now, but I know you do." She never stopped assuming love. After months of working on the relationship and bringing her my regard, I again found my love for her. I know that her continuing love for me was the key factor in this emotional triumph. If she had permitted herself to pull away, our marriage would have ended then and there. Lynda's persistence in loving—even in the face of being unloved—kept my love alive and, in fact, was the seed from which my work in the understanding and practice of love has grown.

Love Does Not Fail

Da Avabhasa, one of my favorite modern spiritual writers, describes perfectly what our response needs to be in the face of feeling unloved. "Love does not fail for you when you are rejected or betrayed or apparently not loved. Love fails for you when you reject, betray, and do not love. Therefore, do not stand off from relationship. Be vulnerable. Be wounded when necessary, and endure that wound or hurt. Do not punish the other in love. Communicate to one another, even discipline one another, but do not dissociate from one another or fail to realize that each one wants to love and be loved by the other in love. Therefore, love. Do this rather than make any effort to get rid of the feelings of being rejected. To feel rejected is to feel the hurt of not being loved. Allow that hurt, but do not let it become the feeling of lovelessness. Be vulnerable and thus not insulted. If you are merely hurt, you will still know the need for love, and you will still know the need to love."[x]

Loving when we are feeling unloved is not done to benefit our partner. It is not a form of manipulation that will produce the love we seek. Moving against our tendency to recoil by bringing loving attention to our relationship frees us from our own unhappiness.

Bringing our regard to those who hurt us is not an act of martyrdom. Loving frees us from our wounds and restores sanity to our actions. By giving our attention we absorb and overcome the collapse that is at the core of our sorrow. Love is the only thing that makes us happy. Therefore, devote yourself to bringing attention, both to yourself and to others. Instead of trying to be loved, love.

Practice Love

A musician client once shared with me a phrase he used to remind himself of the importance of practice.

"If you don't practice for one day you will hear the difference.

"If you don't practice for two days your friends will hear the difference.

"If you don't practice for three days the world will hear a difference."

Loving others is a wonderful concept, but unless we repeatedly put it into practice, our previous patterns of pain will prevail. The ideas presented in this book are like little seeds of wisdom planted in your mind. The potentially life-changing results are enormously meaningful—for your relationship, your life, your spouse, your children, your co-workers, and yourself. These notions will fade away without positive effect, however, if they are not reinforced. We can plant seeds all day long, but if they are not watered, the landscape will remain barren, as if nothing had been sown. Love is only made real through continual practice.

It will not be easy, nor will it feel natural. However, it is only by practicing love on a daily basis that your relationship will be kept new and your heart will remain happy.

Homework: Recognize your mood of unlove. Refocus your feelings by assuming love. Finally, reinforce a more appropriate response to your hurt through the free gift of your attention.

End Notes

[i] Martin, T.C., & Bumpass, L. (1989). Recent trends in marital disruption. *Demography*, 26, 37-51.

[ii] Cookerly, J.R. (1980). Does marital therapy do any lasting good? *Journal of. Marital and Family Therapy*, 6, 393.

[iii] Jacobson, N.S., Schmaling, K., & Holtzworth-Munroe, A. (1987). Component analysis of behavioral marital therapy: Two-year follow-up and prediction of relapse. *Journal of Marital and Family Therapy*, 13(2), 187-195.

[iv] Jacobson, N.S. (1984). A component analysis of behavioral marital therapy: The relative effectiveness of behavior exchange and communication/problem-solving training. *Journal of Counseling and Clinical Psychology*, 52(2), 295-305.

[v] Jacobson, N.S. (1993). Research on couples therapy: What do we know? Where are we going? *Journal of Counseling and Clinical Psychology*, 61(1), 85-93.

[vi] Watzlawick, P., Beavin, J.H., & Jackson, D.D. (1967). *Pragmatics of Human Communi-cation: A Study of Interactional Patterns*. New York: W.W. Norton.

[vii] Gottman, J.M., Coan, J., Carrere, S., & Swanson, C. (1998). Predicting marital happiness and stability from newlywed interactions. *Journal of Marriage and the Family*, 60,5-22.

[viii] Gottman J.M. (1999). *The Marriage Clinic: A Scientifically-based Marital Therapy*. New York: W.W. Norton.

[ix] The Holy Bible: New international version. (1985). Matthew 22:37-40

[x] Avabhasa, Da (1993). The Incarnation of Love: "Radical" Spiritual Wisdom and practical Instruction on self-Transcending Love and Service in All Relationships. Clearlake, Ca: Dawn House Press, 113.

About the Author

Brett R. Williams is a psychotherapist, speaker, and writer whose primary passion is helping couples with Love-Based Solutions™. He has appeared several times on the television program *Reality Check*, as well as the radio show *Issues of Life*. He is also the author of *Xaler and the Dragon: A Relaxation Technique for the Anxious/Fearful Child*.

Brett holds a license as a Marriage and Family Therapist and is Clinical Director of *The Practice of Love*, offering Love-Based Solutions for couples and families.

He has also served at both the state and local levels on the Board of Directors for the California Association of Marriage and Family Therapists. Brett has been in practice since 1989. He has offices in Newport Beach and Huntington Beach, California.

Married for almost 20 years, Brett and his wife, Lynda, have two wonderful boys, Wesley and Trevor.